Aphrodite Emerges

THE JOURNEY THAT CHANGED MY LIFE
AND CHANGED MY FATHER'S TOO

SUSIE HERRICK

ART BY ELLE LUNA

Terdrom Press
Woodacre, California

Published in 2017 by Terdrom Press
publisher@terdrompress.com
Woodacre, California

Text copyright © 2017 by Susie Herrick
Drawings copyright © 2017 by Elle Luna

Publisher's Cataloging-in-Publication data

Names: Herrick, Susie, author. | Luna, Elle, illustrator.
Title: Aphrodite emerges : the journey that changed my life —
and changed my father's too / Susie Herrick ; art by Elle Luna.
Description: Includes bibliographical references. |
Woodacre, CA: Terdrom Press, 2017.
Identifiers: ISBN 978-0-9988702-0-5 (Hardcover) |
978-0-9988702-1-2 (ebook) | LCCN 2017908196
Subjects: LCSH Herrick, Susie. | Self-actualization (Psychology) |
Fathers and daughters. | Man-woman relationships. | Spiritual
healing.|Self-esteem. | Self-perception. | Spiritual life—Buddhism. |
Spiritual life--Tibet region. | Dreams. | Mysticism. | BISAC
BODY, MIND & SPIRIT / General | Biography & Autobiography /
Personal Memoirs | Self-Help / Personal Growth / General
Classification: LCC BF637.S4 H483 2017 | DDC 158.1/092—DC23

Library of Congress Control Number: 2017908196

Editors: Bradford Cottel, Elle Luna, and Christine Moen
Designer: Elle Luna

The text of this book was composed in Adobe Caslon
Printed and bound in the United States
and other countries worldwide
For inquiries, please visit www.aphroditeemerges.com or
info@aphroditeemerges.com

For my Dad
who bravely paved the way for other men
to listen to their wives and daughters

*I have called on the Goddess and
found her within myself.*

MARION ZIMMER BRADLEY

CONTENTS

APHRODITE EMERGES

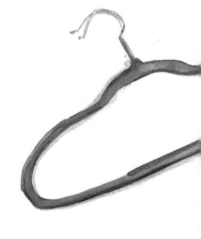

PROLOGUE

The Gawddess dressez ahh twenty pahcent awff," said a voice with a New York accent. I followed the sound and discovered a woman standing behind the register, sporting pale-rimmed, thick glasses and a short haircut, not the usual look of a "goddess" type.

I looked back at the dress I was holding and began examining the mystery that had captured my eye and then lassoed me directly across the highway from our lunch restaurant, to the shop.

I had first noticed its bright green, puffy sleeve protruding from a full rack of items on the veranda at the front of the shop. It just hung there, as if to say, I'll wait while you eat your Chinese food—and then: you're mine.

It was familiar to feel my mind slipping sideways during one of our micro-adventures—my friend and fellow adventurer Pat had that effect on me. And, it was typical of a Northern California day: redwood trees, a bit of wood smoke in the air, clear blue sky, and what I'd call a lingering, ghost-like flavor of hippy utopia.

Goddess dresses? I mouthed silently—with a jaded look—at Pat, who was thumbing through cards on the other side of the small store. I pictured women draped in long, flowing dresses with fitted bodices at new-age events and began to walk the dress back to the rack.

Pat intervened. She was smart when it came to adventure. She got that it was important to follow something when it called to you. She knew that events, like me noticing this dress, were a sign—a foretelling that, if followed, would lead to a sort of predestined adventure ahead. She looked up at me with her mischievous smile and channeled the dress with a whisper.

"Try it on anyway."

Just like Alice's white rabbit, following Pat's whispered command was a practice I would become conscious about later, to "follow the goddess when she beckons, even if you think you might look stupid." Accepting my fate—and I should say my seventy-dollar fate because, as predicted, the dress fit, looked perfect, and left me with no defense—I proceeded to buy it.

The counter was tall and made of glass with shiny things inside the case and on top of it. I lifted my preordained purchase over to the proprietress. We chatted while she wrapped my dress, and the conversation turned to her spouse. On the wall behind her was a small photograph of her and a young man in his forties, at least twenty years her junior and very handsome. I stared at the photo.

"He's my huzhband," she said with a matter-of-fact tone.

Pat and I looked at each other.

"How did you meet him?" I asked, because now I had to know.

The shopkeeper looked at me intently as her eyes protruded above the oversized lenses that rested near the tip of her nose. "I maahnifested him," she said.

Then she pushed her glasses closer to her eyes and looked down at my credit card receipt printing on the machine. I had to somehow come to a silent understanding of her three simple words by relying on left-brain, cognitive processes. I . . . manifested . . . him, I repeated to myself as I strummed my fingers across a pair of long, dangly earrings hanging on a display nearby.

"Manifested him?" I said, trying not to show my disbelief. "How?"

"I wrote a list and read it aloud fohr seven days," she said. "And I used a maahnifesting bowl, just like the ones I have fohr sale, right over there." She pointed to one side, where I could see collections of colorfully painted ceramic dragons and statues of the ancient Egyptian goddess Isis.

"Wow," I said, thinking about the list she'd made and recited for seven days. I had some dots to connect, and I wondered: did it happen just like that? Did he simply appear?

"He was the yawngest of the age range and a widowuh too," the shopkeeper said, "and that's what I'd asked fohr."

She seemed so sure of herself. I felt pulled by the success of her story, and my cynicism struggled for survival. They must have met when she was much younger, I thought to myself, assuming again that there must be a catch.

"How long have you two been together?" I forced myself to ask.

"Three yeeahhs, and he ahdhores me. We ahh very happy."

Surprisingly, she seemed oddly unaffected yet amused at my not-so-well-hidden wonder at how the whole thing could've really come about.

I felt a warm, relaxed sensation enter that soft bundle of nerves just below my ribs. Her story signaled a definite hint of dawn, a slight thaw, after seven long years of despair. Had my dark night really begun to recede because of an ex-New Yorker selling new-age stuff, just off the highway? How could I operate from prejudice when I had found this practical inspiration in the most unexpected of places?

Then the shop came back into focus. As I glanced up, I noticed a tree branch suspended above me, where crystal earrings dangled in the sunlight. I could do this, I thought, as I ran my hand through the rainbow of light reflecting onto the countertop. I could bring more moments like this—moments of magic—into my life. As I turned to collect the dress, Pat was in the process of buying one of the manifesting bowls. Immediately, she turned and handed it to me and winked.

"Here ya go, girl. Go for it!"

I began to protest, but gave up the moment I caught the persistence in her eyes. I stared at the bowl. It had a teal hue and was crafted as a primitive statue that looked like a goddess bearing a hollowed-out, heart-shaped womb—a place, I wondered, to hold the list? I looked at Pat and nodded slightly, in appreciation, and then I looked back at the intriguing shopkeeper still behind the register.

"How is the marriage going?" I prodded, in what I considered a final test. "I mean, how're you doing after three years?" I pinched at the fairytale-like story, rooting for it to be true, not yet believing.

"There ahh a few things I fohrgot to put on the list," she said. "But generally, things ahh goin' well."

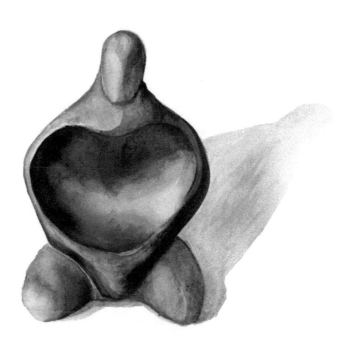

THE QUEST

Aphrodite just kept smiling. Because she was just doing what a goddess does—the same way that a tornado rips houses apart or a fire burns down a forest.

L. J. SMITH

SO FAR AWAY

I raised my hand. I was restless.

I sat in the audience, watching a few men attempt to impress each other. Come on, guys—seriously? The discourse had gone beyond that of angels dancing on the head of a pin—unimpressive to me, to say the least. I wasn't interested in knowing what they thought; I wanted to know what they *did*. Like, how did these men treat their wives?

I had been an observer as well as a participant in spiritual and religious debates over most of my life, and I had come to the conclusion that life was a sort of classroom and that the curriculum was designed to teach unconditional love. I wanted to be around people who were interested in that, not a bunch of men who were making a sport of religion or spirituality: Who was the best meditator? Who knew the most esoteric teachings? And, who had the most realized teacher? Now these sorts of discussions seemed colorless, like that tinny sound of something hollow, with no substance inside.

Suddenly, in my righteous reverie, I was called upon. I cleared my throat and addressed the speaker. Attempting to be respectful, I said, "You're talking about profound concepts related to human awareness and spiritual development."

The room became quieter, and I could hear the sounds of cotton clothing rub across the carpet as many in the audience began to shift their body in search of a more comfortable position on the floor.

"You're talking about how others might become enlightened," I went on, noticing that my voice was getting smaller, and I was beginning to feel intimidated.

"And I'm interested to know if you've personally experienced any of the things that you're talking about?"

I could see large windows that filled one wall behind the speaker. The late afternoon light seemed to soften the appearance of the untamed yard outside. Then, before the speaker could even respond, and almost as if on cue, a small Greek chorus of men belted out in unison, "That is exactly what he is talking about!"

A bit dumbfounded, I looked at them. Were they *all* wearing wire-rimmed glasses and faded polo shirts? I now understood why none of the other women in the room had spoken or raised a hand. What is the use of competing over that?

What was I doing here?

I turned to face the handsome, bald-headed man who illuminated the room despite his casual posture. He sat on the cream-colored carpet, surrounded by his audience. Although I'd not heard of him before, it turned out that he was Ken Wilber, a prolific writer and respected thinker, particularly in relation to the fields of transpersonal psychology and spirituality. Earlier that afternoon, before the talk began, I passed by him and found myself a little surprised by his height, and then I overheard him say that the only ones who argued with him were those who hadn't read as much as he had.

Now, having asked the question, I realized I was in a worse position than those underread challengers because I hadn't read any of Ken's books, nor, I'm sure, even one-hundredth of the books that he'd read.

I prepared for an attack and inwardly began to wish I'd never come to the event.

"Yes," he said, with a warm smile, "I have."

Then—silence. The whole room seemed alert at that point, and I could see the crowd lean in to hear him elaborate.

"One time, I had to get so far away from everyone I knew—so far away that I became intensely desperate, and all I wanted was to just touch someone's flesh," he said with a disarming earnestness, "and only then did I begin to experience it."

I was stunned. I wasn't prepared for his candor or calm enthusiasm.

Furthermore, I'm not sure if it was his expression, how he said it, or the actual content of what he said, but he answered my question. The "it" at the end of his sentence was what resonated in my mind. And, whatever "it" meant, the experience he was describing was clearly something almost tangible, something that I could sense and perhaps recall. In fact, the word "it" activated a mysterious sense of relief for me.

It was then that a man in the audience informed the group that his wife had died six weeks earlier. He said he was attending the event because, just before her death, he and his wife had read Ken's book about the death of Ken's wife, Treya. With a swift and skillful movement, Ken positioned himself across from this man seated in the middle of the room and said, "I don't care what the rest of you do right now, but I'm going to be with this man and focus on him." He reached out with his hands as if, it seemed, to create a small planet of compassion that held us all in proximate orbit. It was then that I realized that, by the time Ken had addressed this man and me just before, the hollow feeling had left the room.

AS LIGHTS OF the nighttime traffic seemed to rush past me during my drive home, I savored the warm feelings I'd experienced in that room, and I began to reminisce. I recalled Ken's relaxed but earnest demeanor and the position he'd taken on the floor, face-to-face with that thoughtful, grieving man, and also the feeling of relief I'd had after Ken had said "yes" to my question about his personal experience. These reflections brought to mind the relieved expressions I'd seen so often on the faces of my students and clients. They were expressions that usually came about when something was said that resonated within their heart, and then they appeared to have been absolved of whatever had been haunting or troubling them—somewhat like a child might appear upon discovering that magic really does exist.

While continuing to drive, I recalled one client in particular who had just that expression. I was seeing his family because his son was on probation. They had been faithfully and happily coming to sessions for some time, and then one day the father became angry and said he felt disturbed by my reflections of his son's complaints about him.

"I'm a religious man," he said, "and I don't believe in any of this psychological mumbo jumbo."

Stunned and ready to defend myself as well as the profession, I remembered I'd been trained for moments like these. He had been hurt and he'd reacted automatically, so I reflected internally: what might really be bothering him? It occurred to me that it must be frightening for a parent to have a child in juvenile hall and then on probation because that meant the parent was no longer fully in charge of the child. The father felt vulnerable because someone else had control over his son, and up to that point in the session, I had control over his son and, for that matter, his role as a father, as he perceived it. So I decided to give him back some control.

"You've been coming here for eight weeks, and something has been working for you because you keep coming back. You are the head of this family. It's your decision. What would you like us to do next?"

With a look of release and some regained self-respect, he said, "Keep on doing what we have been doing so I can talk to my son." I remember noticing how his whole body seemed to find comfort where he was sitting.

In family systems theory, this is called joining with the resistance. It is a way to gain someone's attention and trust by putting that person at ease with a supportive response to his or her perspective. The technique is designed to help the therapist show respect for what someone is saying or communicating, no matter how defensive the person may seem, so that he or she can let down personal defenses. Some call it a verbal Aikido technique, which involves flowing with the energy instead of against it. Ken's reply to my question had that effect and gave me the feeling that I could relax, which made it easy for me to hear him.

"So far away" is what Ken had said. *So far away.* How lovely, I thought: his time for inner reflection and digestion. This was a directive for me. I needed to become quiet to hear a faint voice from beyond, a voice that I had been searching for. Getting "so far away" would be like a form of sensory deprivation, and there is something about being away from the familiar and kinesthetic distractions that would provide me other ways of acquiring knowledge.

Even this time for traveling home in the car offered a glimmer of it, a time to think about what had just happened.

THE NEXT EVENING, I was journaling on my computer about all of these insights along with various other psychological and spiritual knots I was chewing on—including my job situation at the time—when my neighbor called.

"A large owl has landed in your redwood tree, the redwood next to your deck," she said in barely audible low tones. "I believe it has at least a five-foot wingspan." Holding the phone, I walked to the window.

The large owl gripped our tree branch, and I could see just enough to make out its claws. Hunting time was about to begin, I thought, noticing the sunset and darkening of the sky. After our call, I checked to see if all three cats were in the house. It's odd to think of a bird as carnivorous, and this was a big one. It was magnificent. Its beauty, and most of all its ability to fly, touched on a vague feeling of longing in me. I had just been writing in my journal about how I felt stuck; externally for me it was a vocational inertia; internally it felt as though my heart were filled with glue. It was as if I were trying to get somewhere in a dream, but I couldn't seem to reach the destination I wanted.

> *June 22—I am facing my fears. I am afraid of feeling dependent on men, and I want to engineer my life so that I do not have to feel like this.*

I stared at the bird again. Silence.

When I was twenty-one, I fell into a depression after my usual challenge: the loss of a relationship. What became clear to me then was that I had neither a sense of self nor self-esteem. I had totally identified with the thought that I needed to become enlightened and save the world, but at the same time I felt that I was never really good enough to attain that goal.

I left Creative Initiative Foundation (CIF), the religious and educational organization in which I was raised, because it seemed—rightly or wrongly—to be the source of this problem. Initially, I made this decision without really knowing why. Then, I thought I would need a new teacher to replace the organization's authority over my spiritual life. But when I read Herman Hesse's Siddhartha and learned of his decision not to follow the Buddha, it hit me that—no matter how amazing my teachers may have been, which they were, or could be in the future—no one could act as a conduit of the truth for me. Enlightenment could not be attained through someone else's experience. Advice I may get, but to arrive where I wanted to go, I had to become my own authority. I needed look no further than within myself to find meaning in my life and make my own decisions about what was right and wrong for me.

I freed myself from CIF and went my own way, further into

samsara, the everyday playacting of my existence. At that age I had also figured that once I'd found a mate who was willing to work on anything that arose and who wanted to have a committed lifelong relationship, I would require nothing else.

So I was, from the get-go, to become the greatest and best therapist around as well as a fine life partner.

All those childhood years I was involved in spiritual and religious studies, ceremonies, relationship processing, political causes, and meetings with people like Joseph Campbell and Buckminster Fuller should have prepared me for this. In fact, in seventh grade, I was demonstrating about the dangers of nuclear power; engaging in group sessions at our seminar grounds with my peers on the teachings of Jesus in relation to the central themes of all religions, as well as on the subjects of philosophy and psychology; and attending group meetings with my family and others to discuss family dynamics. And now, I had devoted all of my years in school—undergraduate and graduate—to studying relationships.

Well now, here I am, with barely a career, pondering its destruction, and I'm in a marriage that has been worked upon and tended to expertly and lovingly, but it's still missing a small but extremely desirable element: an adult passion.

I watched as one of our cats came to the window when it noticed the owl. I began thinking about the talk and the hollowness I felt there in the beginning and speculated about the connection between that hollow feeling and the lack of passion in my relationship.

It seems that I could maintain my lovely, comfortable, aging life without this passion that wants to live, but my intuition keeps saying, 'that piece is important for your survival!' Even while writing this, I feel dizzy with immense emotion.

I turned to the window again. I feel lost, without a roadmap, I said silently to the owl. Where do I go from here? Silence.

Why are you here? Silence.

Of course I have a bias because I am a therapist.

I wondered if this journal entry were for the bird.

We therapists are an odd lot because, just as popular belief has it, we believe that every aspect of one's life holds significance. Having this belief, along with my serendipitous fall into an academic profession, has reinforced and instilled in me to always have an internal third-party observer. I was trained to interpret. You can blame it on Freud. Well, actually, in my case, blame it on Carl Jung and on my childhood.

An example of this belief in the significance of events—or synchronicity, as Jung would call it—is the root word "ken," or a close derivation of it, in several languages, including German, English, and Scottish, and it means, "to know," or "consciousness," or "range of knowledge." This connection is so fascinating and significant because when Ken answered my question with delight and compassion, I felt that I'd received knowledge and wisdom. He had gone beyond the intellect to tell me how he did it. It was just what I had wanted to know.

Jung was probably the first psychologist I'd ever heard of, and he is still my favorite. His dream analysis was so extensive that—similar to the Tibetans—he saw all of his waking life to be dreamlike, and he interpreted outward events as such. In this sense, every aspect of a dream serves as a symbolic language of the unconscious, and every aspect of our waking lives can also serve us in that way as well. These symbols can help us to integrate our experiences. In fact, everything that we dream or experience has meaning. Each encounter with someone or something can be interpreted within the context of the dream or the context of one's life, as a tool for seeing inside the "self," as it were.

I reached for my *Medicine Cards*, a worn and tattered deck with a book of meanings that I took with me practically everywhere. A friend, who had given them to me years ago, told me he'd received them from a shaman and thought I might find them useful, too. My friend was a physician who, at the time, was working to integrate his own allopathic training with the surreal mystical traditions he'd been encountering. He later became quite successful at this endeavor. Ever since he gave me the cards, I've found them to be one of the most useful mystical tools I know of: the practice of seeing the external world as a series of metaphors for understanding the internal world.

In accord with their traditions, Native Americans see experiences and interactions with animals as metaphors for learning about the self. They consider encounters with animals to be a form of medicine, and they say encounters carry different messages and meanings relevant to the particular animal involved. The cards my friend gave me served as a modern interpretation of these insights.

The deck is composed of fifty cards, each adorned with a gorgeous, detailed depiction of a different animal. One side of each card in my deck had a sky-blue background with a yellow thunderbolt. Sometimes I found it useful to just pull a card on chance, but on this particular day, since I had actually encountered the animal—the owl in my tree—I went directly to the accompanying book to read about the symbol.

"Owl," I said, scanning the book. "Owl," I read, in slanted black calligraphy, "Casting out deception" by seeing through people. I took a deep breath. If everything one encounters has meaning, well then, somehow, to "to see right through" people was in my future. Deception? Oh God. Who is deceiving me? I hate that. I like the cards when they have something positive to say, but when the interpretation is something ominous, it's not my thing.

"Can I fly with you?" I asked the owl aloud this time, wishing I were in that tree.

Once again, the owl spoke with its silence, and then I knew what I had to do: I wanted to follow Ken's advice. My husband was away on a trip, so I unplugged every electronic device in our house and sat in solitude for three days. For just a moment during that isolated, sometimes-lonely time, it felt as if my cells had expanded. I felt a sense of purpose, and two questions formed: Was this the "it"? And, where do I take this next?

Then, as if on cue, the magic arose: my friend Nancy called. "Want to go back to Tibet with me?" she said. "My flight leaves the first week of September."

No matter how intangible, lean into longing;
it's your own voice leading you home.

ROOF OF THE WORLD

But I am not going to live forever. And the more I
know it, the more amazed I am by being here at all.

WILLIAM HURT

The night sky was dark with a waning moon when Nancy and I landed in Hong Kong. We were spending the night before catching our next flight, to Tibet. It felt like torture to be stuck in a windowless hotel room—just as the jetlag hit—and left only to contemplate those final words my husband had issued just before I flew away: "Why don't we separate?" I wondered if this were the feeling I'd have if I were shot while running. I couldn't quite feel it because it didn't hurt yet, but the lethality of the bullet was there, deep down. Shouldn't it really hurt? Shouldn't I be afraid?

I couldn't stop moving my legs around in the cramped bed. What is it about, this tucking in sheets at the end of the bed? How can you stretch your toes?

While part of me was trying to assess the possible damage of his declaration, another part of me became conscious of a long-forgotten sense of release. For moments in this prison of a hotel room, I started to feel suspiciously happy and free. I savored it for just a second, but then questioned whether I should be concerned that this feeling could dangerously overshadow important concerns I might have about the future. Can I truly allow myself to fall into this lovely feeling?

My legs continued to move, and I couldn't find sleepiness. Conflicted about relaxing, I lay there feeling the sheets in that boxy excuse of a hotel room. Even after a thirteen-hour flight, we still had two days of travel ahead of us. I had to get some sleep, and finally did, only to find that morning came too soon. I got out of bed even though my body ached in defense. It didn't want to move.

Again, in the darkness, with our bags in tow, we managed to return to the airport and board another plane—this time to Chengdu, the cheaper route into Tibet. After we landed, we took a taxi to the Chengdu Traffic Hotel, checked in, and then left for a meal at a local restaurant. It was the night before the last leg of our air journey, and we reveled in the final moments of varied menu items and the luxury of a low-altitude setting.

Then, I found myself once again—in a dark room, where I felt pulled to think and attempt to piece together my reality. My marriage was far from fine, yet we had been together for so long, and we had always worked things out. I was going to be loyal for life—even though I was, admittedly, miserable. As I lay in stiff white sheets, my body not quite fitting in the tiny bed, I realized I was afraid of the dark. During the day, I was as brave as the next hearty traveler, sometimes even more so, but at night I was much more aware of my vulnerabilities. I am so far away, I thought. But wasn't that what I wanted? Wasn't that the goal of this whole trip—to get *so far away?*

The yellow streetlights from outside cast a sepia pall over the room. As I lay in bed, I thought about the owl, and I was visited by an image of my mythical hero King Arthur, flying like a bird. I recalled that the mage Merlin morphed him into animals and birds when he was a child, so that he could learn from their perspectives. The compassion that arises from adopting another's perspective seems wise practice to teach a child, I thought, especially one who would grow to be a leader. I chewed on the possibility of deception and felt uneasy. Uneasy and free? What a combination of emotions.

I must have fallen asleep because the next thing I knew, I was waking up again in the dark. We were headed back to the airport for the final leg of our trip. I hated breaking sleep, yet stepping on that dark, naked tarmac in the early hours reminded me of how much I loved adventure. The other travelers had a kindred look, and I felt that we were part of a lucky group who knew that flying to Tibet was a rare privilege and something far better than any screenplay. As if the first scene were opening, the sun rose as we took off and began our ascent.

Taking three flights to get somewhere is a lot. But the last flight there made it seem almost painless. We flew east, over Sichuan's green forests, famous for their rare giant pandas, passed by the snow-capped peaks marking the beginning of Tibet, then the barren lands where yaks graze, and the rivers that find their way to other parts of the vast Asian continent. The rivers are the perfect metaphor for understanding the immensity of the place. Life-giving water that supplies nearly half of the world's current population of well over seven billion is sourced on this rooftop of the world, the Tibetan Plateau. Billions of humans are fed by this essential, life-giving and life-sustaining element that flows from this generous land.

As we touched ground and entered the country's familiar yet exotic surroundings, a lovely yet odd feeling emerged, a feeling a bit more than the blissful, adventurous state I was used to experiencing while traveling: I was filled with grace.

I HAD BEEN to Tibet once before, when there were hardly any cars, and even in the cold winter air then, we rode bikes everywhere. Being in buildings that lacked heat was a new experience for me, a Californian. For long periods, the temperatures were sub-freezing, and it felt doubly strange to walk into an occupied dwelling or building and find I could always see my own exhalation. I kept expecting relief from the cold, but found absolutely none—anywhere. On the surface, at that time, Lhasa was a sleepy, quiet place of the Chinese army. And it was a Lhasa of the past, a place where dogs roamed everywhere and most of the native people still wore traditional Tibetan garb. The elaborate, pueblo-style buildings stood alone for the moment, safe from the future "modernist" additions of white tile and blue glass.

This time, as I entered Lhasa again, it was four years later, the height of the Clinton era back home, and just a month after Princess Diana and Mother Teresa had died. Lhasa had become an intense city, whirling with taxis, new businesses, and many Han Chinese inhabitants, and it was strangely warm. The arrival of Internet cafés punctuating every corner was just a few months away, and El Niño was in full swing at home. Where were the dogs?

After being in Lhasa for a few days, I figured out where I wanted to go. Nancy needed to stay for work, so I was free to pursue my journey solo. There was an appealing place called Terdrom, the site of a hot spring, about a day's journey from Lhasa, and that seemed to me to be an ideal spot to go to meditate and explore.

Before I took off, I felt ready to contact my husband. I wanted to let him know that I understood his desire to separate and that I could let go. After all, I thought, we are best friends. We can separate and be free and still be close. We lack sexual chemistry, we've had no passion for years, possibly ever, and now we'll each be free to look elsewhere.

We'd been relying on faxes and phone calls, but when Sandy said I could use her email account to contact him, I felt great relief at not having to call him. I wrote my first-ever email, and, to keep up my courage while typing it, I remembered that I was on a quest: I had received clues from the owl, and then Nancy had called at just the right moment. What I did know for sure is that I just couldn't let myself lose the magic. Synchronicities were everywhere, and while I felt that I was doing something potentially dangerous by ending my marriage and stepping into the unknown, I was feeling grace and the power of freedom and movement, and I was enjoying it. For me then,

Tibet seemed even more magical than ever. All my feelings seemed amplified as I hit the "send" button, which in some way finalized the old, my past, as I anticipated the new.

If this were a children's book, I could almost see a Tarot reader seated in an armchair, in another dimension, turning over the "Fool" card, the card that means the one who draws it, or is dealt it in a reading, is about to blissfully stride off a cliff and be catapulted down, into the depths of the psyche. Would I have stepped off this cliff had I known the precarious uncertainty that lay ahead? At the time, the cloud of my excitement obscured my perception of the cliff.

I made a new friend at the Yak Hotel—a young Israeli who carried what was barely a backpack. Unlike him, I wasn't in seasoned traveling mode, and I'd packed much too much, which made traveling even more difficult. My new friend and I had agreed to hitch a ride to Terdrom, but we got stuck walking a chunk of the way there. After a while, we found rides and eventually reached our destination, a spread of small fairytale-like buildings standing before a backdrop of striking cliffs.

Terdrom is an ancient Buddhist pilgrimage site—one of the places where, long ago, Padmasambhava hid secret esoteric treasures. Padmasambhava, also known as Guru Rinpoche, was the meditation master who had brought Tantric Buddhism from India to Tibet in the eighth century. Now pilgrims and other travelers visit, and like the resident nuns, chant and meditate, and soak in the hot springs.

Then, as if to add to what seemed a surreal state, snow fell one night, and we awoke the following morning to see the yaks breathing steam and shaking layers of snow off their fur.

I walked around the houses below the cliffs and visited the nuns. We exchanged the customary white silk scarf, called *khata* in Tibetan, which is offered to a recipient who accepts it and then generally returns it to the giver by lifting it over the giver's head and placing it around his or her neck, as a blessing. The nuns served me tea and I gave them writing pens I'd brought from the States.

As I sat in the springs with the pilgrim women while they washed and re-braided their magnificent black hair, I observed them as they artfully interwove the strands with semiprecious stones of turquoise, amber, and coral. Their red cheeks and pearl-white teeth were stunning against their dark complexion. I was in heaven.

One day there, I witnessed a young nun who, with a face obviously contorted in pain, was persistently pressing her fingertips against her temples, so I gave her some aspirin in hopes of helping to ease her headache. We played my travel flute and exchanged some very basic words. Then, true to the frequent fate of a naïve traveler such as I, the next day it seemed as if the entire pilgrimage population, dressed in their black wool coats with brocade lapels, arrived with excited breath at my small doorstep. At first, they held out their hands in anticipation of receiving the aspirin they'd heard about, which I didn't have much of. Our encounter felt a little awkward for only a second, but what I did have was an outpouring of new love blossoming forth from the big crush I was developing for the place.

We all stood together at my door for some time, simply acknowledging the wonder of each other's presence. After offering the few words I knew, all I could do was simply be with them in my delight. How could I feel any other way? I asked myself. I was a popular novelty with these pilgrims and nuns, who, to me, seemed far wiser, more grounded, and better equipped to deal with adversity than almost anyone I'd ever met.

A week later, I met a spiritual seeker from Mount Shasta, California, and he and I discovered that we shared a mutual dear friend named Marilyn, who, for me, had been a guiding light throughout my life. Synchonicity was everywhere. We were sitting in a nun's home that was filled with richly carpeted benches and hand-painted chests. The nun there was housing Westerners because the guesthouses in the hot springs were full. My new Mt. Shasta friend wore a purple Tibetan-style coat with an orange sash—uncommon colors even for

Tibetans. He leaned over and asked me, "What are you doing here?" as he proceeded to stare at me and then added, "When you were talking with the locals, I saw 'Christ-light' shining down on your head."

"Excuse me?" I said, confused.

"Yes," he said, with a gentle kindness. "As you spoke, I could see a beautiful, otherworldly sort of light coming through and descending onto your head."

I simply thanked him for the compliment and headed to bed. But sadly, my cynicism threatened to take over and ruin the buoyancy of the magical feeling I'd been experiencing. This man reminded me of the old world of my childhood, a new-age world that was full of magic and possibility, a powerful world that I'd relished when I was young and craving spiritual experiences. Men of this sort had enchanted me back then, but by now I'd become wary of them and would ward them off.

When I returned to my room, I looked at myself in the mirror, wondering exactly what it was this man had seen. As I saw my reflection, to my surprise, I also saw the light of my face glow like so many of the Tibetans. Suddenly, I felt unmistakably expansive. Was there really something here that brought this about? Was this why travelers ventured here—to experience a light, an energetic understanding, of something beyond our readily knowable dimension of life?

People ask, Why Tibet?
I tell them, you can get a better view from the Roof.

DECLARATION OF POWER

Traveling outgrows its motives. It soon proves
sufficient in itself. You think you are making a trip,
but soon it is making you—or unmaking you.

NICOLAS BOUVIER

The next day, I returned to the Yak Hotel like a dharma puppy full of the hubris of a born-again Tibetophile. "I get it, Nancy," I said, breathless, when I saw her. "I get why so many people are in love with this place!" We grabbed a table at our friend's restaurant and, as she smiled at me, I saw a small familiar female figure dressed in pants emerge, silhouetted against the kitchen lamps shining behind her. "Tashi-la!" I said joyfully, standing up to respectfully take her hand. Tashi was a savvy entrepreneur, Nancy's touchstone in Tibet, and my very wise friend who was already gesturing to the young girl working for her to bring up two plates of our favorite: banana pancakes.

Typically, women at that time in Lhasa wore the traditional chuba, a dress or long coat, but not Tashi. She looked understated and practical, which made it easy to underestimate her. Her plain clothes framed her dark skin, black hair, and white teeth. She had the most radiant smile. She had been an aristocrat, but now she was just another Tibetan trying to make ends meet. She spoke English while not many locals did. Westerners adored her. She always wore a pair of simple black trousers, an oversized cardigan, a Spider-Man pin she'd obtained from a Western friend, and a turquoise scarf that I had given her. The uncharacteristic style of the pin struck my funny bone, I guess, because it wasn't clear why she favored it or wore it. It was just something that stood out, with no evident explanation.

A few years had passed since I had loaned Tashi a beloved scarf my husband had given me, and she wore it as protection for what was then a persistent cough. I consider turquoise to be a powerful color, and I wanted to somehow be of help to her. "Here," I said to her at the time, removing the scarf from my neck and handing it to her. "It's the color of communication from one's heart. It will heal your throat. You wear it."

She received it, as is customary in Tibet. But I never expected her to actually wear it regularly—not for four years, anyway. It was a scarf from the Gap, and it had matching gloves. And, despite the many gifts she had received from Westerners, there seemed to be something about this object, something that was very important to her.

"I get it. I get it," I said to Nancy and Tashi as we were eating the hot pancakes. "It took another trip for me, but now I get what everyone is talking about. I get why you keep coming back to Tibet. You're in love. I'm in love."

Nancy just smiled and ate while our friend Sandy, who was a physician with the United Nations World Health Organization (WHO), joined us. "Let's go to Lake Namtso!" I said.

But Nancy said she was too busy with work and had to decline. Sandy agreed to go, and within a day or so, we had the adventure planned. Tashi boiled eggs for us, two of my new travel buddies went to gather supplies, we hired a driver with a Land Cruiser, and we all prepared ourselves for the adventure just ahead. After we packed the last bag, Tashi and Nancy waved us goodbye, and, just before I hopped in the car, I spotted Tashi's Spider-Man pin on her lapel. I smiled at the superhero and felt within me the sort of energy that could take on the world. I was ready for my next adventure.

After a long day with a lot of dust, bumps, and stops for noodle soup, we crested the pass and drove down to see the lake, which was a refuge for pilgrims, travelers, and large raptors. Namtso is remarkable with its huge size, unusual caramel and sand-colored rock formations, and graveled shores. Spiritual pilgrims gather there and carve prayer mantras into stones they find in small caves along the lakeshore. They chant with the sounds of the wind and crunching gravel underfoot as they circumnambulate the lake.

When we arrived, we found a small building, which was a gonpa, or Tibetan meditation shrine or hall, on the lake. We dumped our bags in our room there and shook off the vibrations from the Land Cruiser ride as we ran to catch the twilight.

The lake was still, and the stars were barely out. The sky glowed with a dark teal that was reflected in the lake, while monks and nuns in meditation formed a rim along a small portion of the lake's edge. Their crimson robes swayed to and fro in the slight breeze, but their radiant bodies were like living statues of stillness and silence.

I was surrounded by beauty and quiet and reveled in my anonymity. I was far away from any expectations as well as much of what I realized I normally depended upon. I've had such a magnificent life, I thought as I approached the water. I was finally feeling empowered, as if my life were my own and my marriage a cocoon that I'd now left behind. I had always sensed a strong, sovereign core inside me—actually something even more recognizable than that—a woman with no self-doubt and no hesitation: one with a complete freedom of being.

As I searched the horizon for the other side of the enormous lake, I noticed a bright star in the sky. Unlike all of the other stars, this one didn't seem to twinkle. Its light was strong and clear—ahh, I thought to myself, there she is, the planet Venus, planet of the divine feminine, the planet of love. This force, this co-creator, inspirer, helper Venus—could she guide me? I asked myself.

Throughout my life, I'd heard stories of voyagers and pilgrims who would pray in order to receive answers or visions for what to do with their life. Something about Venus called to me—and this planet representing ancient feminine wisdom began to fill me with power and strength, which I felt for a moment as I looked toward her. Intuitively, I felt that this was my chance. Kneeling in the gravel, I looked up at this bright light, with my eyes closed, my heart fully open, and I surrendered in prayer and said, "Okay, whoever is up there, I am ready to learn. Teach me. Teach me how to become enlightened."

Then I prostrated devoutly, in the traditional Tibetan way, lowering my full upper body to the ground three times. Now, unbeknownst to me in my elated state of mind, it was there, in that moment, the moment that I would scream about later, where it seemed that I had signed my life away and had entered a full-time mystical boarding school that never allows anyone to go home for vacation.

Be careful to whom or to which planet you pray! For my call was heard—whoosh! All the ethereal paperwork was waived, and I was in the program: let's destroy Susie's ego.

Over the next seven years, my prayer would be answered—in painstaking thoroughness. Furthermore, Venus, the planet of the divine feminine, would create a special series of tasks just for me, it seemed. This was the beginning of my path into the labyrinth of my life, a journey into my own center: the place that was the truth of who I am; the essential me . . . which has always been.

I have often contemplated if this were how Icarus felt when he took to the air on his winged flight, or how Arthur felt when he first created the Round Table. I was literally high in elevation and emotionally high, too, with the feeling of my prayer being heard. It was then that the wax on my wings started to soften ever so slightly. The challenges began almost immediately.

DARKNESS

When the gods wish to punish us,
they answer our prayers.

OSCAR WILDE

now began to fall in the night, and it didn't stop. We were
trapped at Lake Namsto for three days. On the third afternoon,
our driver took us to the pass thinking he could get us out,
but he failed in a tenacious flurry of spinning tires on ice. We were
prevented from going up and over and decided to spend the night in
our Land Cruiser, in hopes that the weather would clear enough by
morning to allow us a crossing.

Four of us shared the back seat, two were in front, and my young
Israeli friend, who had never before seen snow, sat behind all of us on a
jump seat, farthest back. Travel adventures bring unexpected closeness
with strangers, and here the quarters were really close. It was not a
warm night, and the occasional Tibetan nomad would trundle by,
and, if curious, open our door to get a peek at us, the cold, "stupid"
Westerners who, shivering and awake, were immediately hit with the
resultant blast of cold air.

One of the travelers was an older woman from Israel. She asked
us if we'd ever read "zee book" *Alive*. Between the book and the movie,
everyone was familiar with the plot: an adventure gone awry, where
the survivors had to eat those who didn't make it, in order to stay

alive. In her thick accent, she said, "If zeece happens, you can eat me first." I believe that was the exact moment when I decided I would hike out over the pass the next day, with or without the group. In that small space, those of us within earshot of her looked at each other and blinked. It was time to go.

In the morning, a few of us geared up to hike out, and our Land Cruiser was still stuck. It was a 17,500-ft. pass, and had I known that my estimate of a fourteen-mile trek would turn into twenty-five-plus miles by the end of the day, I would never have started. Three days prior, I had been filled with power at the edge of Lake Namtso, and now? With each step upward toward the pass, my lungs made me feel like I was in a never-ending sprint.

It was longer, colder, and steeper than anything we'd imagined or could've planned for, and then, as the day wore on, all those physical challenges grew even stronger. I had an uncomfortable sense that the experiences of the entire trek—the snow, the wind, and the memories of shivering in the car the night before—were all metaphors for the hardship that was still ahead of me.

"You could have been killed," a friend said to me a few days after we had successfully made it out of the blizzard and across that pass. "Many Tibetans and yaks died," he said as he rested his back against the colorfully painted wall of the Snow Lion Restaurant. He was a doctor, and he confirmed something I'd feared—I had frostbite on my face.

It burned even more as he winced at my appearance and delivered the diagnosis. I gently pressed against the bubbling skin on my chin. "I didn't realize that," I said. "We just wanted out." What I didn't say, but wanted to, was that in spite of the danger and pain, *I did it*—and *I felt adept.*

A FEW DAYS later, I packed my bags to head home. I still felt vestiges in me of the woman whom I had caught a glimpse of at the lake. The adversity was invigorating and more intoxicating than my safe little life back in California.

Finally home, I waited at our house for my husband, Chuck, to return from his business trip. There was a strange piece of new soap in the bathroom. It bugged me. When I finally saw him, I struggled to breathe deep. I felt that familiar block in the area below my ribs. It wasn't until right then that I realized this feeling had completely vanished while I was away from him. But now it was back. My strength started to wane, and I felt sick. Something about being with him made me feel nauseated with fear, as if I were in a sticky quagmire.

For safety, I unconsciously reached for a turquoise bead at my neck. I was reaching for Tibet. I recalled Lhasa and my friends. Huge vistas and lake views filled my heart, and a feeling of freedom emerged along with internal sounds of the wind and the songs of Tibet. I was free from him then, and now I could feel it. Venus was in the sky and I was safe. I was a character in my own epic; he could not take me away from myself. He could not take away my feelings of freedom and self-esteem. I had power. I held the turquoise again and realized I was ready—ready to leave this marriage.

We began the surreal conversation on our cushioned Indonesian bench. The day happened to be Halloween. As I told him about my adventures, I felt like a different person from whom I'd been as his wife. Maybe there was a slight holding back on my part—or maybe even a release from the role. My own voice sounded different to me.

I presented him with the gift of a Chinese gong that I had hand-carried back for him. He was in his suit, and his face looked puffy as it brushed against his white shirt collar. He appeared happy and sad at the same time. We talked about how to finalize our separation. He cried and looked at me with a painful expression that I took to mean he loved and understood me, and then I supposed he was crying because he didn't want me to go. It was as if he were starting to feel the bullet. I took his cues that the time had come for me to fly solo. I felt for him, but not enough to change the flow of my plans. I was moving out.

However, no sooner had I moved out than did the grief move in. I discovered that I didn't have the stomach for ending my marriage, nor did I have the courage to be alone. I was unprepared for this. A friend told me, "Your cells and those of your partner remember each other, and it takes at least three years to recover from such a psychic shock to the system. It feels like the cells in your body are getting torn apart." That's exactly how it felt. I was miserable, the sort of miserable you experience when you begin to come down with fever and find there is no place where you feel comfortable. I craved the comforts of my old life. I was losing my best friend.

Bizarre and nightmarish incidents began to crop up. One day, I went running in the park and found a dead body. Another day, I went to my doctor for a checkup, and she thought she had found a breast lump. On another, I called my husband's office to get his insurance information, but his workmates said he was not there, and they would not share with me how I could contact him. He was in Paris with a girlfriend, I learned later. He already had a girlfriend! That strange soap when I'd returned home . . .

When I tried to date, I approached single men in whom I was interested, and they thought I was too old at the age of thirty-five. Married men would come on to me, assuming that I wouldn't notice their wedding ring or care about their status as a husband. It seemed like all of the movies out at the time were about women being left at forty-something. The recurring theme seemed to be about them accepting that they were going to be alone—forever—whereas extremely old men and much younger women would find each other inevitably and irresistibly attractive.

One day when I looked in the mirror, I saw that I had aged about twenty years in a month. I saw wrinkles, many wrinkles. My friends thought that I was insane, but I knew what I saw. It was really happening, and I became obsessed with the idea that I looked old. The gods were taking away the one thing I'd foolishly thought I could always count on for power: my looks. The most ghoulish, shallow woman entered my heart. She set up a comfortable home for herself, and despair settled in at the same time.

All the gods did was laugh at me. The world confirmed my nightmare: a cashier asked me if I wanted the senior discount at Ross Dress for Less. When I was with a friend, who was one year older than I and was carrying her newborn baby, a young woman asked her, "Are you the mother?" and after she nodded, the woman turned to me and said, "And, are you the grandmother?"

CHUCK AND I entered therapy to either ease the separation or perhaps get back together. I felt terrified all the time and wanted to go home. He would show up at our sessions a half hour late and then talk about how he was the responsible one and I was not, which implied that I was some kind of flake, or idiot. I asked him if he wanted to reveal any secrets; I told him that now was the time to talk about them. On one occasion, he yelled at me, saying, "I've been faithful to you for fourteen years. *This* is the problem in our relationship, Susie: you've been so suspicious of me."

His routine of lateness and accusations repeated itself, and finally one day when the therapist and I were waiting for him in that usual half hour, she turned to me and asked, "Why are you here?" I was shocked at her candor. Somewhere in the back of my mind, I was grateful to her.

"You're never going to have your needs met by this man," she said, and then she continued by saying something that was the opposite of how I thought I was coming across. "You are a talented, beautiful woman. What are you doing with this man?"

It was an unusual yet kind thing for a therapist to say. Looking back, I am now more aware when someone risks something and says something out of character in an attempt to help; it is wise to pay attention. If I'd been in my right mind, I would have filed for divorce right then and there. Yet I only felt extreme loss and the draw to a comfortable past; his treatment of me made me feel more alone. My soul would have to take in the information and process it at another time.

Your gut knows,
Your head resists,
And your heart is
Idiosyncratic.

THE FALL

Half gods are worshipped in wine and flowers.
Real gods require blood.

ZORA NEALE HURSTON

As the weeks turned into months, I searched for release from my pain, only to find mirages of safety and love. Every date and its ensuing conversation started out as a dream, only to become a nightmare behind the ephemeral promise of relationship. Buddhist traditions have a name for what I had become—a hungry ghost. Somewhat like ghouls, these beings are continually attracted to or in pursuit of something that will never satisfy them. No matter how much they try, they can neither obtain nor be satisfied with the elements they desire—but they keep trying, incessantly.

Hungry ghosts are often depicted with pencil-thin necks and empty, distended bellies, a sign that they're forever starving and unable to ingest the nourishment they never stop craving. According to Buddhist tradition, their plight is an example of a particular state of mind experienced by beings that remain obsessed with attempts to fulfill all manner of insatiable desires.

For solace, I crawled back to Tibet and Nepal in search of the magic I had felt there. I was an addict looking for that original high. There was no consolation, just more nightmarish men, and more reflections of the Hollywood paradigm of young female beauty and older male privilege. During the day, I was in the planning stages of establishing an orphanage in Tibet, but I could barely sleep through the night.

The last layer of any illusion I might have had in this regard was torn away when I visited an Internet café in Nepal, thinking it would cheer me up to catch up on some emails from home. What awaited me was an email from Chuck confessing that he'd cheated on me. The cheating began five years prior to our split, when he became involved with a woman who'd taken the job of housesitting for us from time to time.

"She's angry with me," he wrote, "because I'm dating someone else now. She's threatening to write you." He wrote the letter as though he were a victim, and he expressed that he felt that I would understand, since we both knew that there was no passion between us.

I printed the email. I was in shock. Instead of the usual emotional block, I felt actual pain below my sternum. When I was a kid, this was the spot my karate instructor referred to as my solar plexus. The idea was that if you attacked this area of an aggressor's body, it would knock the wind out of that person and thereby disable him or her as swiftly as possible. Now my solar plexus was responding to intense emotional kicks. It became difficult to breathe.

I realized later that when I felt stuck in my solar plexus area, I was mirroring what was, in fact, happening inside Chuck. He was emotionally shut off—he had to be in order to deny the truth and continue his lie. He was literally blocking his own energy from flowing through his body, and I could feel this emotional shutoff. I was learning something remarkable about my own body that was not unlike learning about a great feature of a car I owned, a feature that I hadn't previously realized I had. My solar plexus was a barometer that measured the emotional processes of others.

Chuck knew that I could read him. On one occasion early in our marriage, he said that being with me was like being naked all the time.

Similarly, I had received feedback from others that when they were with me, they felt that I could see through them. Once, a marriage and family therapy intern I was training had told me, "Sometimes you don't want someone to always be able to see through you. It's uncomfortable."

It took me years to understand that I had an empathic ability to kinesthetically feel what was going on in others. My intent gaze and presence in conversation made it impossible for others to hide, not only visually but also emotionally. It was a form of intrusion for those who had something they didn't want seen. When I became a therapist, I found that I could use this ability to help my clients better understand themselves. In psychology and in therapeutic contexts, this phenomenon is called countertransference, which, if used correctly, can be beneficial for a therapist looking to understand and help a client.

If I felt something in a strong way when my clients walked into the room or at any time during an interaction, I began to understand that somehow they were unconsciously transferring their own internal world to me. My challenge was to learn to distinguish my stuff from their stuff. However, if my stuff were triggered in session, it told me that there was something emotional in them that, in turn, triggered me. So when I am with others now, I consciously check in with my body to see what it's registering and then work with that.

The mystery was this: Did Chuck consciously shut down this part of himself so that I wouldn't know the truth? What a skill he had, but what a nightmare he was hiding. Did I mean to say he was hiding it from himself, or from me?

I went back to my hotel room. It was a moonless night. All the stores were closed and the carts were gone or draped with tarps, like coffins. I couldn't bear it. I was so utterly alone. I was scared. By then, I'd been in a dark night of the soul for six months, and all I wanted to do was go home and pretend that none of this had ever happened.

I called Chuck and pleaded to his voicemail, "We can work this out." It was hungry-ghost madness. I was grasping after my illusion, and I felt safe in my denial—the most dangerous of defense mechanisms.32 Its beneficial effect is only temporary, like a drug, and then later, when you can least afford to, when the stakes are higher and the consequences more serious or dire, you have to face whatever you've wished to avoid. Chuck was no longer there—only his voicemail. And eventually there would be no more news, no new emails, and I would be left alone with myself.

The Kathmandu hotel room I'd previously entered with such delight became a tomb, of sorts. My marriage was an illusion, and that illusion had deflated like a large, old balloon landing on the floor, distorted and lifeless. There was only one thing left to do: cry. The desk clerk heard me sobbing, and came up to my room to "help." But the ploy, like the balloon, was empty because then he tried to hit on me. I asked him to leave, locked my door, and listened to his footsteps fade as he descended the stairs. Later a young Western woman knocked on my door and offered to help, which was sweet. Yet there was nothing she could do because there was no help then, only the assimilation and integration of the realities of my life. I cried and cried, sobbing like a child, and I couldn't stop.

There was a time a year later when I saw someone crying like this. She was a very young Tibetan, on a bus. Her husband had just been killed, and she and her parents were on their way to see a great *lama*, a spiritual teacher. She cried continuously for two full hours, all the way to the gonpa. The bus passengers just sat while she sobbed. I understood why they did this because offers of help to someone in that state are useless. You can only be present with them and a witness to their grief. I was amazed at how accepting this culture was.

AFTER A LONG route through Thailand and then Germany, I returned to stay at my parents' home, where I'd left all my belongings. As was oddly predicted, what was waiting there for me was a letter from "her." As I began to read it, I got the feeling this wasn't the letter Chuck had feared. Her words were full of regret and sadness in a simple and direct apology. "I am so glad you know," she wrote, adding that I could call her if I needed to. He must have told her that I knew. I wanted to hear everything, so I called her from the orange phone that still lived in my childhood bedroom. I sat on that old bed and stared at the cedar walls while she spoke. The night was growing dark.

They'd started the affair five years before, and she'd been waiting for him to divorce me ever since. A flash of memory came to me about the one occasion she'd stayed at our house for a number of days, after she'd fractured her leg. At the time, I thought it strange that she had asked to convalesce with us when she didn't know us that well. Then another memory surfaced that compounded the already-broken feeling in my chest. There was *another* woman staying with us one weekend while she had been recovering. This other woman was on a business trip, and, according to Chuck's description at the time, she was "a friend from business school."

"Were there any more, other than you?" I asked her.

Yes, she confirmed: he *had* had two lovers in the house with me at the same time that weekend. It was an avalanche. My suspicions had been real, and the denials of those suspicions expertly done on both his part and mine. How could I ever want to believe that someone whom I loved and lived with would betray me—especially when I had totally committed myself to being on his side and backing him up whenever needed? How could one ever take that kind of deception in? And why would *he* even admit it to himself? The response he'd had once, years earlier, to another of my suspicious inquiries about one of his many female "friends" now stung as I remembered him say with such warmth, "I could never do that to you. I love you way too much."

"What else?" I asked her.

She had become pregnant and had had an abortion, which added yet another blow to my wounds: it meant they'd had unsafe sex. In what seemed like an endlessly silent pause, I began to imagine her in a waiting room at a clinic, and I was curious if she'd been alone then.

"Did he go with you," I asked slowly, "to the abortion?" I glanced down and noticed my jagged fingernails.

"No," she said. The response jolted me. "He told me that he needed to be with *you* that weekend."

For a brief instant, I actually thought to myself, who is this guy, the kind of guy who would do that? Oh, right, I remembered, this guy is my husband, not just some jerk of a boyfriend. Again, silence.

"You should protect yourself," she said. "He hates you. He wants you to have nothing after the divorce."

In my heart, I knew that she, who was just one of the many "other" women, was telling the truth.

This was my fall from the sun. It scorched me and I fell. My wings melted, and the hubris I'd had, with the idea that the world loved me and that I would not be betrayed, was all lost in the dizzying trail of my descent. The demons would have a feast tonight, and if they'd had pain for lunch, they'd be having utter despair for dinner.

Truth does set you free.
But when your illusions
Are holding you up, be forewarned:
The loss of ground is immense.

HUNGRY GHOST

Do you know the most surprising thing about divorce?
It doesn't actually kill you. Like a bullet to the heart or a
head-on car wreck. It should. When someone you've
promised to cherish till death do you part says "I've never
loved you," it should kill you instantly.

FRANCES MAYES

BARDO

That very morning I lay in bed for what seemed like hours, trying to summon enough will just to stand up, and all the while I was feeling anxious. There seemed to be nothing more to me then than a middle-aged harpy who continually grasped at her own image in the mirror to see if the wrinkles were real. Not eating, wearing black. It became uncomfortable to sit, and especially to sit still. Constant, nagging thoughts played on repeat.

I am a cliché. No one will believe me because I seem crazy. No one could possibly believe that I didn't know about the affairs. No one will ever get the depth of the betrayal I feel because this happens all the time. Hate me? Why did he hate me? He was the one having the affairs.

The most terrifying of my thoughts and feelings, the one that regularly and prematurely jolted my body out of sleep, was the fear that Chuck was going to annihilate me. I felt that not only was he going to kill me but that he was also going to somehow "destroy" my soul, which seemed far worse than death. As the long process of divorce paperwork began, I feared that my feelings were actually reasonable and justifiable, particularly when friends shared that his anger was growing to absurd levels. I could easily imagine that in his fantasies he would want me dead. While these feelings seemed extreme, I believed he had the anger and capacity to do just that: annihilate me. As though I were receiving wisdom from another dimension, I knew I needed to protect myself. But with what?

If the metaphor of the mountain pass had seemed daunting before, it was nauseating now. The beginning of the end of our marriage ushered in a horrible blizzard of terror. Eventually, I would be entering into a divorce proceeding against a man who had epic revenge on his mind, and, what's more, a résumé of abilities proving he could accomplish it. To the outside world, Chuck was the paragon of success and intelligence, with an impeccable Ivy League education at Yale, an MBA from Stanford's Graduate School of Business, and a family with the same pedigree to back him up. Behind the platinum appearance, he was a pathological liar, and as already mentioned, according to one of his many paramours, he had been planning to divorce me for at least five years. I felt that he not only wanted to win, but that he wanted to destroy me in the most painful way possible. He wanted to destroy the truth with his anger, and I believe he thought that, somehow, it would work.

My friends tried to help but were horrified by the ashen look on my face. Understandably, my mother wanted to put me on meds, and I wanted to be anywhere but in my body, although I didn't believe in drugs—not for where I was. Everything was pointing to the fact that, for some reason, I couldn't digest or even ingest the truth. No, I couldn't ingest the truth. It was as if I'd eaten rotten food and my stomach was trying to figure out what do with it.

As the divorce paperwork continued to accumulate, I went back to Asia and into a retreat center, or gonpa, with other Westerners, to find solace and peace of mind. But there was none to be had. Here, in this neutral, monastic place, I had to fight the deadly sins of envy and despair and a mind that would not let up. Muttering to myself like someone suffering from schizophrenia was a strange experience. One day during a silent period in retreat, I sat on the rooftop of the gonpa and tried to eat a sandwich while still having the lingering feeling of intense sadness in the pit of my stomach.

As I sat, an eagle flew into my face. It clawed at my cheek and then flew away. It seemed so surreal and yet even this beating from wildlife felt familiar. Was there a worldwide conspiracy against me? Did my husband pay all these people, and now even large raptors half the globe away, to drive me mad? Hot tears ran down my cheeks. I felt mad and inwardly, in a screaming whisper, I yelled at God, or whoever or whatever seemed to be torturing me inside: this is getting absurd!

A COUPLE OF days later, I broached the topic of my emotional state with a small group I was taking part in during this teaching retreat, when I asked a question about my grief and the uncanny effects that seemed to be following me. The group leader was a young man from L.A. who had learned to speak Tibetan. The feeling of my clawed cheek still smarted as I addressed the group. In an effort to deflect any judgment that might come my way, I tried to be as alert and left-brained as possible with my question. "Could you tell me more about what the Tibetan Buddhist thought is on strong emotion? I'm experiencing so much grief that I can't meditate. All I can do is cry," I said.

We were sitting on a small hill overlooking the smoky valley. Images of my depressed clients came to mind, and their disability had now become a kinesthetic experience for me, and as a result my compassion for them was at an all-time high. I was hoping he, or one of the group members at least, would respond with some empathy, but instead, our young group leader, in his L.A. vernacular, said, "If you read the scripture in the original Tibetan, the Buddhists think that, like, grief is selfish."

The group members gasped. I stared at him to see if he was just a

cartoon character. Were his eyes actually rolling? Confused, my fellow
retreatants attempted to say things to soften what he'd said, but it was
just not possible. In victimized outrage, after the group had dispersed,
I marched down the hill to get a second opinion and to complain to
someone in charge. I met with a nun named Ani Karen, an attractive,
middle-aged Swedish woman.

She was plainly dressed in crimson robes and had small bits of new
hair growth on her mostly balding head. The whiteness of her skin
was a bit of a culture shock for me because every *ani-la* I had spent
significant time with had been Tibetan, not Caucasian. She was very
clear in her presentations during the retreat, quite convinced of this
way of life, and now I had her attention. Her eyes matched her clarity
and they appeared surprisingly receptive to me. I felt that the stress in
my life during that time was constantly preparing me for dealing with
being judged, especially being judged by men and Western Buddhists.
But with Ani Karen, I felt none of it.

I told her what had happened with the L.A. guy, and she laughed,
saying, "He's just a boy." I was not prepared for this and thought to
myself, Then why are you having him lead a group? Nevertheless,
when she asked me what was going on, I dropped that thought and
explained the nightmare that seemed to be following me everywhere.
How was it possible that men in other countries and on distant conti-
nents would be saying such similar, terrible things? I admitted that I
probably seemed like a cliché here: an almost middle-aged woman with
a *mala* a and men problems; nonetheless, the nightmare felt painful
and uncanny to me. As I spoke, she was attentive and quiet. After I'd
finished, she reflected on what I'd shared and offered some of her own
recollections.

She told me about her decision to leave Sweden and become a nun
in a small monastery just outside Kathmandu. She said she cried every
day for an entire year. And, each time she went to her teacher and said
she wanted to leave, he would tell her the same thing: "Just stay one

more day." Ani-la paused, and I soaked it in. I imagined her working through all of her feelings while her teacher waited patiently, as if to say, I am here with you while you go through all of your reactions because they are normal, and they are part of the process. Something had transpired for me in that moment. I received what she was teaching: compassion.

Then she said something that, to this day, has continued to significantly change my perspective from that of a terrorized victim to a pilgrim: "It sounds like you are in a *bardo*."

Bardo?

I'm in a bardo?

Now that's something I hadn't considered. I left that conversation with my mind newly fed. This is what I assimilated: a bardo is the Tibetan Buddhist word for the transition time between two states. The most-often-discussed bardo is the transition during and after death and before the next step in the process toward gaining enlightenment or taking rebirth in form. It is a time when all that was not integrated in one's life comes, or appears, before one. In other words, all that you have not dealt with—particularly your own negative emotions and habits—resurfaces, in the form of all sorts of symbolic figures in many guises, and your job is to figure out how to integrate all of that, to recognize and accept that, as a part of yourself, the display of your own mind. In his book *The Tibetan Book of Living and Dying*, Sogyal Rinpoche says,

> The word 'bardo' is commonly said to denote the intermediate state between death and rebirth, but in reality bardos are occurring continuously throughout both life and death, and are junctures when the possibility of liberation, or enlightenment, is heightened.

What happens in this transition time is a bit mysterious and difficult to grasp. In Charles Dickens's *A Christmas Carol*, Scrooge goes through a bardo one night when he is haunted by ghosts who remind him of his past, present, and future. Only when Scrooge is able to see and accept his miserly ways can he change his life—and he does.

Another example of a bardo occurs in the movie *The Matrix*, where Neo, the hero, is hunted by Agent Smith, who represents to Neo all that Neo cannot stand in the world. What's worse, Agent Smith seems to know everything that Neo does, as if the agent's entire job is to stave off the hero to keep him from discovering his own power. The entire movie is essentially a bardo for Neo. Eventually, Neo overcomes Agent Smith, his computer-generated shadow, not by destroying or killing the agent, but by diving into his core and merging with him. When he accepts his arch nemesis as a part of himself, he discovers his true power and is thereby released from the illusion that the Matrix creates.

If indeed I had been in a bardo, as Ani Karen had said, that would mean that all my experiences were reflections, or manifestations, of my own unresolved internal struggles. Like Neo's Agent Smith, it seemed as if this shadow nightmare were following me everywhere. I considered: What was I not seeing? And what had I not yet integrated? As I looked at all that I could not stand about the world, I started to clearly see that there was definitely something unresolved about my relationship to men.

Much like the eagle clawing at my face as I sat on the rooftop of the gonpa, men seemed to swoop down into my life and leave me with a visible scratch. Throughout my personal history, men had treated me poorly, but now I was trying to figure out if something inside me had allowed that as well. Like Scrooge, I went back in time and returned to the edge of Lake Namtso. I saw myself prostrating at the edge of the deep, teal-colored lake, and I heard my voice call out to Venus, asking for enlightenment. Yes, it had all started at that moment of bliss, that peak experience. I put together the whole experience, and I understood that I was, most certainly, in a bardo.

It wasn't for some time that I would learn more fully what this meant and how, in this way, I had been getting somewhat of a Tibetan Buddhist education, and it was neither from a teacher back home nor with books in hand. As I'd requested of Ken Wilber that day at the seminar, I wanted practical knowledge that I could directly apply to my life. At the time, I didn't recognize that I was getting just that, practical ways revealed on a journey of my own creative adventure as I stepped through my valley of emotional pain. It was as if I were drawn to wandering around the Himalayas, carrying too much emotional pain to consciously learn these lessons in other ways. But I was given wisdom pearls that would later rest atop the plush Tibetan carpet of my memories, visible enough and within reach when I needed them. This education seeped into me like hot water infusing tea leaves.

My bardo was now becoming a more conscious experience, and, like any character in a story, my pain was the taskmaster, unrelentingly demanding and poking at me to expand and be free. I felt like Psyche, who was handed a series of impossible tasks by Aphrodite because Psyche had fallen in love with Eros. The process felt painful and unfair, yet I—like Psyche—was being secretly helped by the other gods that took pity on me. One of the greatest "messengers of the gods" for me then was my friend Tashi.

ONE EVENING, I was having dinner in Lhasa with fellow traveler Glenn Mullin, a scholar and longtime student of dharma who had written over twenty books on Tibet and Tibetan Buddhism. I asked him, "What is it that keeps you coming back here? What is that golden thread that you keep following here? What is the draw?"

Aware of his track record for doing in-depth research, I was prepared for a long explanation, a treatise, as it were, on the benefits of Tibetan culture, but instead he gave me a very simple answer.

"It is the state of joy that one naturally comes by here," he said. And then he went on to say how he'd seen it in the most ordinary of places in Tibet. He revealed an astonishing account of his adventures and dangers, and I was envious.

"You seem to have no fear," I said. "How is it that you have no fear?"

He told me of an accident he'd been involved in when he was just nineteen—an incident that, I assumed, had occurred in his native Canada. He'd been hit by a truck and then thrown from it—another near-death experience, or so it seemed to me later.

The next morning, when Tashi and I were drinking sweet-milk tea at a sunlit table in her restaurant, I recounted this story to her and commented on how fearless Glenn seemed. "Once you give yourself up, you will feel no fear," she said. "You discover pain is not the same as unhappiness.

"Unhappiness is caused by the mind, and, of course, there are a lot of causes for unhappiness. And, likewise, there are causes that make you happy, and those causes also depend on your mind," she said. I supposed Glenn understood that, and that perhaps that understanding provided him with some degree of freedom from fear. Tashi seemed to think so.

I told Tashi about the bardo explanation that Ani Karen had given me. Tashi explained that bardo experiences are often frightening because, although the experiences aren't actual material things, their appearances can seem, or feel, very real because they manifest in the mind.

Our bardos are ghost-like places—in fact, some Tibetan Buddhist practices are done in graveyards, in order to help prepare the practitioner to face illusory appearances, or experiences, and to have compassion for all that appears. What makes those appearances feel solid and real is our fear of them, including our fear of those things that appear to transgress us during these transition periods. It's also the pain and struggle that we feel when such things arise.

However, according to Buddhism, it is compassion—the temporarily veiled component that is our inherent nature—that acts as the catalyzing agent, which we can learn to cultivate as we grow in right intention and understanding. Compassion allows us to see that others transgress us only because they, too, are in pain and don't really know the actual essence of their own inherent nature. What we might see as conflict is, in reality, illusory.

One might say, simply, that compassion is the understanding of suffering, and that when cultivated, compassion naturally bears witness to, or embraces, suffering and does not judge it. When we can develop compassion and learn to extend that to whatever we seem to fear most—whether we recognize that fear to be arising from within us or we think it is triggered by something external—we are in that way also extending compassion to what is most painful or difficult to accept within one's self. As we continue to face these difficult and sometimes nightmarish states by learning to cultivate naturally open, nonjudgmental awareness, we come to see our fear with insight, through the strength of compassion.

According to contemporary psychological thought stemming from Jung's work, eventually we come to "integrate our shadow" and wake up to the dreamlike nature of our lives. This is similar to the process of traversing one's bardos—like the bardo immediately after death. To make it easier to traverse this bardo after death, Tibetan Buddhism teaches us not to grasp after a deceased one, particularly at the time of his or her death, and then during the traditional forty-nine-day period that follows. It is said that if the dying one is able to maintain awareness at the time of death and during the period that follows, he or she will have an opportunity to awaken.

Buddhist philosophy encourages us to support those who are in the process of dying or have died by holding positive thoughts, love, and compassion in our heart. Tibetans believe those in the dying process as well as those in the transition periods, or bardos, that follow need all the concentration and focused stability they can muster to successfully cross over unencumbered, to move through "the valley of the shadow of death." Pulling, or grasping, at a person in the dying process with one's emotional attachment only prolongs the person's suffering and robs that person of the concentration, or focus, he or she deserves and needs in order to grow or attain freedom during this critical transition time. One's grasping onto the dying person can easily prevent him or her from achieving a good death, and it may also block his or her release from the traditional forty-nine-day bardo that typically precedes rebirth.

I needed all the positive thought I could get, and no pity. In the Tibetan tradition, even the dead are given this sort of respect for their journey. This was the path to enlightenment, Tashi said. But while this method seemed easy to understand, it was difficult to practice. As John Muir said,

> But when I heard the storm and looked out, I made haste to join it; for many of Nature's finest lessons are to be found in her storms.

Because of these pivotal conversations about bardos, I knew that my path was to step directly into the bardo of my own life, to acknowledge my feelings and experiences, and to welcome the ensuing adventure, no matter what seemed to appear. I would do this in order to come to an understanding of what I resisted or couldn't accept about myself—whatever I wasn't acknowledging or was trying to push away or somehow hold onto or possess: my delusions.

I was beginning to understand the meaning of this metaphor for death, the meaning of the bardos in general, and possibly why the seventeenth-century Japanese Zen master Shido Bunan had said to die while you are alive. Giving up the idea of a separate self and realizing the true nature was what I wanted to do. And, I stood in awe: how did

Tashi know this well enough to immediately recognize this process unfolding within Glenn?

I knew Tashi's stormy life was a bardo as well, and, in contrast to her struggles, I realized my own looked like a light summer drizzle. I knew she'd seen the worst of life, but I didn't know the details, and I don't think I could possibly ever know the depth of all of her experiences. Similar to Psyche's final task to go into the underworld—from which, it is said, one cannot return—Tashi had definitely gone to "the valley of the shadow of death," so to speak, and had seen the underworld.

ONE DAY I asked her to tell me her life story. I had often felt an almost palpable sense of spaciousness emanate from her. I thought that if I could learn from her how she had survived, I could, in turn, learn how to thrive myself. We met on several occasions to do just that, and I enthusiastically wrote every word that I could capture. I felt her story was an epic of epics, and I was enraptured with every moment of it. After a while, she would shyly approach me with a little giggle about this storytelling and say, "Let's get back to my humble life." I knew that she was saying let's go talk, which was a relief because I realized that perhaps she was also receiving something powerful from sharing her story.

Mostly we sat together over tea. Several times, we sat outside, and she wore a lovely white hat. I was pleased to see her comfortably seated in a chair, with her body relaxed and a smile that revealed her pearl-white teeth. Some of the most precious times of my life were at these times when I'd hear about her hardships, her loves, the glamour, and the tragedy—all of which she seemed to perceive with a heart filled with love and compassion. Tashi recounted these things to me during those days: she was the product of a love match, she said. Hearing that made so much sense to me. She glowed.

Tashi's mother was seventeen when she gave birth to Tashi out of wedlock, and Tashi's father was heartbroken when it was arranged for her mother, who was his love, to marry someone else instead of joining his family. At that time in Tibet, it was common for two brothers to marry the same woman, and Tashi's father and his brother were already both married to Tashi's mother's sister. While they considered bringing Tashi's mother into her sister's family, Tashi's family decided that, despite her mother's love for her father, it was actually best for her mother to marry someone else. They were all aristocrats, and Tashi's mother was a great niece of the 13th Dalai Lama. In fact, Tashi's mother's brother was a minister in His Holiness the 14th Dalai Lama's government, in Lhasa. Even her father was the fourth-ranked government official who worked in the foreign affairs office of that government.

I imagined tall, handsome men in those yellow silk Tibetan robes or chubas, with their long hair arranged atop their heads. At that time, their days were likely filled with walking the streets of Lhasa, visiting various palaces, and attending to His Holiness the Dalai Lama. In fact, Tashi's father visited the United States in 1948, as part of an official delegation of the Tibetan government.

After Tashi's lovely young mother married, she bore another daughter with her new husband, but tragically, her mother died during that childbirth. It was a sad day, and Tashi was returned to her father's home, and her newborn sister was left with her own father. Years later, I learned that Tashi's aunt, who was still alive and residing in Berkeley, had said it was Tashi's maternal grandmother who had insisted that Tashi's mother marry someone else, and that she (Tashi's aunt) had wished that they had let them all be together in her household, where Tashi's aunt was living and married to Tashi's father and his brother. It was a surprising admission coming from the woman who bore two other children with this man who was her legal husband. Yet she knew that his heart was with her sister, Tashi's mother.

When Tashi was young, she was educated in India, where she

learned English with her half brother and sister, who were her aunt's children. When Tashi returned to Lhasa, she was to be married into another aristocratic family, but she resisted emphatically. Tashi wanted to be a teacher and did not wish to be married. Yet, traditions were upheld and her family won out. She was also married to two brothers, like her aunt; however, it was the older one she was to be with (as the younger one was only fourteen at the time of their wedding). On her wedding night with the elder brother, Tashi said she was so terrified, she grabbed hold of the braid of her maidservant and kept a tight grip on it for hours that soon turned into three entire days. Eventually, Tashi was able to consummate the marriage with her husband, and, over time, the story became one of those legendary family tales told over a litany of giggles. Her older husband was around her age, and they soon fell in love. She said it was then that life seemed blissful for her: they had a son and all seemed well.

Then one day, when the family was picnicking beside the Lhasa River, tragedy struck: Tashi's older husband suddenly drowned. Startled by that story, my mind moved to the scene Tashi described, on this great river that was home to yak-skin boats and pebbled shores. As she spoke, I could see them all, dressed in their dark wool chubas and gathered together near food that had been spread over bright carpets that lay atop an area of the small stones, and perhaps they had set up a blue and white sun tent for shade in the bright, high-altitude sun.

In my mind, my main visual was that of Tashi as she stood along the river, watching and waiting in terror, hoping for her husband's rescue. As this tragic story goes, he was caught in rapids and a whirlpool so strong that even his servant, who dived in to save him, also drowned. Their bodies were not found until days later, and Tashi said she was beside herself with grief. Once they'd been found, she said, she entered a state of shock, which, by her own description of it, sounded to me like a mild form of catatonia. She was so far removed while in this stupor-like state that, despite many efforts from her in-laws and her other husband to rouse her, they remained unsuccessful.

But after some time, Tashi's surviving husband (the younger of her two husbands), had an idea to conduct a healing ceremony for Tashi while she was in this catatonic state, and the ritual involved a piece of turquoise that his brother (her recently deceased husband), had worn as an earring. Tibetan men often wore a piece of turquoise attached to a red thread that had been pulled through a pierced earlobe. It was believed that this particular turquoise piece held the "spirit" of Tashi's deceased husband. Accordingly, it was with the power that allegedly emanated through this opaque, blue-green stone they used in the ceremony that, somehow, Tashi returned to consciousness as her catatonia dissolved. The surviving brother, who had become her sole husband at that point, had revived her.

It was then that he and Tashi went to an area of their land, in a place called Phari, to undertake a meditation retreat and also afford him with time to study for civil-service exams he was required to pass for his forthcoming appointment to His Holiness's government. Although Tashi's surviving husband was still young then, because his only other living brother—who happened to be older—had become a monk, Tashi's husband now became the family patriarch.

Following that retreat, Tashi and her husband returned to Lhasa, where her father's family had grown very concerned about the delicate political situation in Tibet. They requested that Tashi join them in leaving Tibet immediately. But Tashi told them she wanted to remain there, with her husband's family, so she watched as her father, her uncle, her aunt, and her two half-siblings departed for India in 1959.

As His Holiness was being secretly escorted away, Tashi's surviving husband was one of the men who attempted to defend Tibet by securing the south gate (he was now a government official) of Norbulinka, which had served as the traditional summer palace residence and surrounding park for the succession of dalai lamas since the late eighteenth century; however, Tashi's husband was captured, which resulted in their separation for some time.

At some point she was separated from her son as well, who was forced to live on the street at the age of seven, when she herself was taken away. Not long thereafter, her son suffered from serious malnutrition and ensuing illness and soon became critically disabled. Tashi spoke of her son in the context of our earlier conversation about hardship and traversing bardos. Due to others' transgressions, her son had been rendered permanently disabled, but he was eventually given some medical help.

Her son's medical challenge was the one thing she could not reconcile within herself, she said, and she continued to experience deep grief over his disfigurement. To me, it seemed shocking that she had no anger. I was blown away. "How were you not afraid and angry all the time, Tashi-la?"

She explained that Tibetans don't have a habit of complaining because they believe whatever befalls them to be a result of their karma. And they see that when one person transgresses another, he or she is really transgressing his or her own parent, so to speak, because all creatures, according to Buddhist belief about reincarnation, have at one point or another in the vastness of time served as one's own mother or father. So, essentially, there is no separation.

"We hold them all with compassion," she told me.

WITNESSING TASHI'S COMPASSION was humbling for me, and it shed light on what had been my own inability to find compassion for Chuck. I was starting to see what a beginner I was. My problems were like walking down a well-paved street in comparison to her rocky ascent of a metaphorical Mt. Everest. She knew loss and grief and she knew forgiveness, compassion, and real resolve. I am so grateful for the wisdom that has been cultivated, preserved, and transmitted from the profound Buddhist spiritual tradition of Tibet.

One of my favorite moments with Tashi occurred on what was a common sunny day in Lhasa. I was once again at her restaurant, enjoying a banana pancake, when she inquired about me, and then, with a tone of great care, disclosed to me that she had heard from her daughter about my divorce. While, at first, I recoiled upon recalling that very painful memory, I felt the strength of her compassion touch me.

"It pales in comparison to the horrendous travails you've endured during your life," I said. "And I am embarrassed by my grief and anger over something that seems so trivial."

"Betrayal is always extremely painful, no matter what the context may be," she replied.

We were together at one of the tables, where I remember Tashi sitting very relaxed, in a dark sweater and pants, as an angle of bright sunlight streamed through a nearby window and highlighted her shiny black hair. I remember her glistening white teeth that accented the golden hue of her native Tibetan complexion, which, even at age sixty-three then, was smooth and beautiful. "Thank you, Tashi-la. You are so kind," I said. I was grateful to have her in my life and longed to give back in some way.

She was dying even then.

The turquoise scarf that I'd given her was wearing thin, but she still kept it with her. On that day, I noticed the meandering configuration in which it had fallen just beside her on the bench, and I recalled that the meandering path is also one of two basic features of a labyrinth. Similar to the structure of the human digestive tract or to patterns one can easily see replicated throughout nature, which are often found in ancient drawings, the meander is a metaphor constructed in a symbolic physical form that represents the spiritual journey, or path. The other feature of a labyrinth is the spiral, which is about going inward, journeying internally.

The labyrinth has an ancient and varied history among many cultures across time. It represents a more feminine approach to the spirit, a process that is not straight and direct, but rather, one that takes twists and turns—and, more important, time—time to reflect, to learn, to digest, to understand, and to savor the process rather than the goal. I knew this message was surfacing at the time, in that moment, from a wisdom and source within me, and I sensed it was from a time long gone, a time before patriarchy. I was puzzled: why hadn't I connected to this before?

I looked down at the scarf overlapped in folds that spread over the bench, and I thought about Tashi and how she had learned to practice a remarkable patience for dealing with the continual tragedies and hardships that arose throughout so much of her life. Bardos—these transitions—seemed to me to be a recurring pattern, or cycle, of experiences that keep returning to the same place, but often at a different level. "*Rey*," she said, "it is like how we learn more about compassion on deeper and deeper levels." *Rey* is a Tibetan expression denoting affirmation, or agreement, such as "yes," or "it is." I agreed: it is the path to learning.

Tashi smiled and wrapped herself in the turquoise scarf. Later, she would give it to a beggar who was in need of warmth—a fitting ending for that comforting accessory that had been so well loved.

After eons of holding court in the unconscious,
the Shadow is well aware that a declaration of power
sheds light on its hiding place and, if left unchallenged, could
weaken, paralyze, or destroy it. As the shadow realizes
it is naked and exposed, it is forced to engage
you in a battle. A battle with a ferocity
far beyond any that you believe you can endure.

SACRIFICE

I have been in Sorrow's kitchen and licked
out all the pots. Then I have stood on the
peaky mountain wrapped in rainbows,
with a harp and sword in my hands.

ZORA NEALE HURSTON

I stared out from yet another jet plane window. I was heading home, to deal head-on with my own current bardo, which, on one level, meant legal documents, hatred, and courtrooms.

I had to consciously face all that I had tried not to see before, in order to find a way to wake up enough to protect myself. In my mind and my journal writing, I sifted through the past to try to remember all the ways Chuck had lied to me and had blamed me for things that, in fact, he was actually doing himself—things about which he had pretended that my accounts were untrue and my suspicions were unfounded when, instead, the events had actually occurred as I had suspected. The thought of facing all this triggered a horrible nausea that I felt rise up from the core of my gut. No matter how much I tried to tell myself that this was not a life-and-death issue, just a divorce, and tried to find compassion within myself, I simply could not find any internal strength and certainly no empathy for my husband.

My father had once told me that when I was with Chuck my power "went away." Now I was at the core of this powerlessness; I was helpless and without any hope.

I WAS DIVORCED on the connubial chopping block, in a pro tem courtroom in the Marin County Civic Center, an iconic design of Frank Lloyd Wright. I watched Chuck take what he wanted—he was seemingly an expert at this, but how was that so? The house became a symbol of his triumph, as though he had slaughtered an evil dragon. He had made sure he was the one man who did not have to give his ex-wife the home. He claimed legal dominion over everything and seemed to have succeeded in making me look incompetent.

This is not supposed to be happening to me, I said to myself, not after all the years I've spent saving the world, working on sustainability, resolving conflict, and working on my relationships; no. To come to this moment of total failure made no sense to me; there just wasn't any logic to it. But my body knew that the game was over and Chuck had won. To wake up one day and learn that the man to whom I had so deeply committed myself would be so blatantly devious and unfair in his conduct and in our separation would end up the victor, regardless of the cost to me, was indeed a stripping away of the delusions I had that I would be somehow saved by the truth of his behavior.

"What has happened to the world?" the kid in me demanded. "Will the liars always be the ones who succeed? Where are the angels? Where are the good guys?" I looked around and could only see judgmental, impatient faces. It wasn't about the truth.

It was a bardo indeed.

The pro tem judge ceremoniously acknowledged the date of our wedding, the date of our divorce, our current names, and my new name (reverting to my birth name). The sound of his voice in its trance-like state was so similar to the sounds of the voices of those who read us our vows at our wedding that it felt as though this judgment were a sort of bookend ritual, somehow predestined to follow the church ritual we had enacted all those years earlier. I was sandwiched in time, looking at what lay between these two moments, the birth and the death of our commitment.

It was then that I felt my body react as if it had a mind of its own. My tears refused to be dammed; they just kept coming. I couldn't stop crying, and I fought the sobbing, but my body convulsed, mercilessly.

Then something very distinctive—more than just a daydream—materialized before me. While the judge continued to speak in his low tone, like a headmaster declaring an academic expulsion, I kept seeing a horse. It was a brown velvety mass of muscle and sweat that was emitting blowing, breathy sounds. It was trying to break free, but it was being sacrificed. All of the power, life, and loveliness of this magnificent creature was being destroyed while it was having its throat cut at some gathering of self-assured professionals that included my self-righteous husband.

The image was so clear that I wanted to cry out. The relationship itself was a living being. All the beauty of it—the moments of insight, vulnerability, love, shared experiences, and growth—would be taken away in that moment of terror that had been preceded by all those fierce expressions of greed over mortgages, cars, desks, and retirement funds. This deeply impressed upon me then that ceremony itself—like that marking a marriage—is a form of spiritual technology that can breathe life into a new entity.

Now another form of ceremony was delivering the deathblow, with those presiding functioning as executioners and demanding a ritual sacrifice to the gods of ownership and self-protection. The horror and majesty was terrifying yet awesome. I knew the magic was there, and the realization that our divorce was also affecting another dimension in such a profound way was overwhelming. The event brought back an ancient memory. It felt familiar, this vision into another world that seemed to lie just beyond my understanding.

The judge's face returned to my view when he asked me if I understood what he was saying. Again, I realized that I was the one seeing my life break apart before me while the judge and lawyers uncomfortably shuffled their papers about and were already beginning to think about the next case.

The curtain lifted for a moment, and I was the only one who could perceive this magnificent animal and its harsh demise. While still attempting to mediate my tremendous gush of emotion, I acknowledged the judge with a wild nod. By that time, it had become clear for probably everyone in the room that I'd come to personify all that they disdained, and all that was ineffective, and that I'd concretized their inability to accept our vulnerabilities, weaknesses, losses, and certainly, our grief. With that nod, I had embodied the horse in its moment of death.

I was no longer able to summon any will or agency. All that was left of me seemed to be water and the shaky sensation that can follow when one has just seen magic. Later, I wondered if that is the nature of the bardo—to render one incapable of relying on anything that seemed to work before to make a change.

IT WAS MUCH later that a colleague of mine interpreted this sight as a gift from the Goddess. This gift, my ability, had always been there, but I hadn't realized that others didn't experience events in a similar way— nor had I sensed just how far apart this ability had set me. In my heart, my colleague's interpretation felt right, even though in my head I had dismissed it as superstitious or not scientific—merely a daydream. Luckily—in my role as a therapist—I knew the power of this type of imagery. Having an image as a tool to work with was a way to begin to transform a difficult psychological process. It wasn't until much later that I became willing to concede that another dimension was quite close at hand for me. Whether it was an archetypal experience from the collective unconscious or a magical gift from the Goddess, I now felt I had conscious access to a world that others could not or would not see.

Barn's burnt down—now I can see the moon.

MIZUTA MASAHIDE

VICTIM TO PILGRIM

Ged stood for a long while there on the pavement. At last he looked at
the old man who waited inside. "I cannot enter," he said
unwillingly, "unless you help me."
The doorkeeper answered, "Say your name."
Then again Ged stood still a while; for a man never speaks his own
name aloud, until more than his life's safety is at stake.
"I am Ged," he said aloud. Stepping forward then,
he entered the open doorway.

URSULA K. LE GUIN

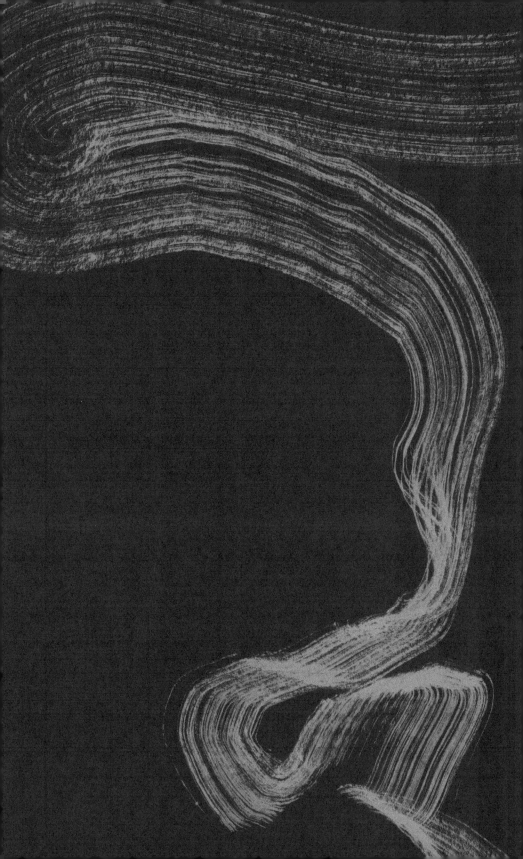

CALL OF THE CONCH

The journey to one's own shadowland is arduous, and it takes all the energy one has just to stay among the living. Despite all the glow of the world around me, I experienced an ever-present sense of gloom. I couldn't escape the sensation, and it reminded me of a low-grade virus that never goes away.

At one point, enraged—mad at the universe for torturing me—I shrieked, "Turn off the fucking learning tap!" to whatever or whoever I thought could be somewhere up in the sky. "I am soooooo done with this pain!" I was done done done—*done*. I was done being rejected, done feeling like an idiot, done with always saying and doing the wrong thing, and, most of all, I was done with not being loved. I felt sick of the nightmares—the sleeping ones as well as the waking ones. I wanted to go home to my old life in Marin, to go back to Chuck, who would say it was all a bad dream.

Instead, I hobbled back to Asia again, only to continue to confront the demons that were occupying my mind. They haunted me with a merciless quality reminiscent of the stories I had heard about dakinis. These beings, translated as "sky-goers" or "sky-dancers," were, according to the Tibetan Buddhist tradition, a feminine force to be reckoned with.

In the Vajrayana tradition of Tibetan Buddhism, dakinis appear in many forms and contexts as spiritually realized female yoginis or women with extraordinary potential, sometimes *mahasiddhas* in their own right, and they often assume the role of spiritual partner or consort of a male yogi or *mahasiddha*. The Tibetan word *khandroma* denotes a dakini in human form, characterized as having a wrathful, or even volatile, temperament. The poking and painful prodding of my psyche caused me to ask myself if the dakinis were hell-bent on getting me to understand something.

I mused on this for a while, until I ran into a real one—a human being who, as legend has it, is the embodiment of a dakini. I met her in late spring, when I was with an American man who spoke fluent Tibetan. He went by the name Yongdu, something his teacher had given him.

Our magical adventure began one day when we decided to walk to take in the views from upstream. We found ourselves alone in a paradise of wild irises punctuated by an occasional yak herder singing or whistling to himself as he passed through the area on horseback.

One of the things I truly love about Tibetans is that they'll sing anywhere. When I was staying in Lhasa, on another trip, I heard a young man singing at the top of his lungs while operating a jackhammer in the street just below my window. Even when I was trekking in Nepal, I found it easy to distinguish Tibetan hikers from others just by hearing their songs.

After attending one festival, I joined a whole busload of Tibetans on the return trip home, and we all sang in unison, no matter the age. Not long after we began the return trip, our bus had a flat tire, so the driver and another man headed off to repair it, while the rest of us deboarded and headed for the nearest field of mustard grass, where we danced together in circles as we resumed our singing. By the time we returned to the bus, we were all short of breath. I watched the bright, radiant faces of all the Tibetan men, women, and children. Their cheeks bore a crimson flush that accented their pearl-white teeth, and on their heads they wore wreath-like crowns of bright yellow flowers.

But now, back to the paradise of wild irises in the field with Yongdu. As we stood listening to the water and a yak herder's song resounding from beneath cliffs that jutted out in a greyish-brown formation, the scene reminded me of a Maxfield Parrish painting. We found a spring and determined its water was potable, so we cupped our hands and drank from what appeared to be an alive and moving glass bubble surrounded by small bright leaves and grasses set in rock and shale.

I stood up again and gazed across the horizon of distant peaks and a wide spread of grassland to my left, where yaks and horses were grazing. Then I turned back and scanned the ravine where we had walked. As we settled ourselves on the grass again, just to soak in the moment, a young, little monk, who seemed no older than eight years, approached us. He moved deftly in his crimson robe, with his right arm bare and hanging free of the folds of cloth, in keeping with the Buddhist monastic custom. We could hear the red fabric move with the air and flap against itself as the child quickly ran toward us in his great excitement at seeing travelers.

Yongdu spoke to him in Tibetan and then turned to me and asked if I wanted to see the gonpa. Now on this spectacular day, visiting a smoky black room full of butter sculptures and lamps, after already having seen so many of those kinds of places of worship, was not really what I wanted to do. So I replied with an honest no, and Yongdu agreed that the splendid day deserved our worship simply in and of itself, and so he declined the invitation for us both. The little monk stood there a bit longer, in silence, and then offered something else in Tibetan—something, it seemed, more tempting.

"He wants to know if we want to meet the Khandroma," Yongdu said as he turned to me, using the Tibetan word for dakini, or female master.

I stared at him in pleasant shock. She—the Khandroma—was the most mysterious female *rinpoche* that I knew of, and it was said that she was usually in some kind of very long, secluded retreat. Rinpoche, a term of endearment that literally means "precious one," is an honorific reserved for highly regarded, reincarnated lamas in the Tibetan Buddhist tradition who have gained significant spiritual accomplishment and are often highly learned.

In her previous incarnation, where this Khandroma was known mainly through legend and the tradition of whispered lineages, it was said that she had the ability to fly through the air. I'd only read about her and was told that only a few Westerners had ever met her. So there was no question: I had to see this "living buddha"—the first one I'd heard about and would ever likely see in my lifetime—who was in female form.

So we followed this little fellow while listening to the flapping of cotton folds as the wind rushed through his robes. He led us up and down the grassy slopes and through a literal hole-in-the-wall portal to a hidden valley. I smiled and imagined a Tibetan version of *Butch Cassidy and the Sundance Kid*. When we finally found our footing at the base of one of the hills, we were instantly awestruck with what came into view directly before us.

THERE SHE WAS, allegedly one of the most famous women in Tibet, Drikung Khandro Tenzin Chödrön—Khandroma, for short. She was considered a living emanation of Yeshe Tsogyal, who was an eighth-century saint and the first enlightened buddha to appear in female form in the Tibetan tradition. Yeshe Tsogyal was also a consort of Padmasambhava, or Guru Rinpoche.

As we approached, Khandroma was standing atop the mossy roof of a new retreat hut being built for her. She wore a sun hat that matched her robes, and eyeglasses with lenses that darkened or lightened according to the amount of exposure to light.

A huge cooking pot, or cauldron, filled with what the Tibetans call "Milarepa stew" stood just behind her. Greenish in color due to its chief ingredient of nettles, the stew was the primary food that the legendary eleventh-century Tibetan saint Milarepa ate while he was deep in retreat for many years. One can easily identify him in a Vajrayana thangka painting because he is depicted with green skin and an emaciated look due to his diet of nettles and ascetic lifestyle.

Two huge ravens stood behind the cauldron and Khandroma. Regarded as good omens, ravens were often the harbingers of an inexplicable and unfolding mystery. Cauldrons were known to serve not only as large cooking pots but also as containers for formulating alchemical magic. When I saw the ravens, the cauldron, and this woman who had the spiritual fortitude of a mountain, I took it all as a sign that my intuition and prayers for release into this adventure were doing their work.

Despite the fact that I was in the patriarchal cultural tradition of Buddhist Tibet, whose history has been dominated by males, these were arguably powerful symbols of feminine spirituality, not the male-centric versions more commonly found there. How wondrous that these symbols were situated there, on the roof of the world, and right beside this extraordinary woman appearing directly before us while her next meal simmered in the warm sunlight.

As we sat with Khandroma on a grassy, rocky patch of earth, she began speaking to Yongdu. My mind jumped forward, and I wondered if she was planning another retreat and if it would be another ten years before anyone would have an opportunity like the one we were experiencing just then.

"She is asking about you," he said.

I was touched and also feeling a bit overwhelmed. I looked at her in those normal-looking, thick glasses and the odd maroon sun hat. Her stature was impressive, nothing diminutive, and she looked like she was used to being treated with respect. I thought to myself how I would seriously love to see if she could fly.

"She says you are like a dakini and that you can cut through the ego with a knife."

Yongdu translated this last sentence with his eyebrows raised. I looked at him, actually stared at him, and then gazed out to the wide expanse of green grassland to attempt to understand the meaning of what she had said.

"Cut through the ego with a knife?" I said as I looked back at Yongdu again.

"Yes."

I reached under my turtleneck for a necklace that a friend had given me; suspended on the chain was a small representation of a curved knife, in the shape of a *drigug*, or traditional dakini knife, and it was only at that very moment that I began to learn of its symbolic purpose. I gazed out over the peaks and the small clouds scattered among them.

Yongdu said, "I told her that you would take refuge with her as well."

With that, I gave Yongdu a fierce look. He had me in a corner because technically I had said before that I *would* take refuge, under a very specific condition. In an earlier retreat, my fellow Western retreatants kept asking me if I was going to do it.

Refuge is a fundamental and significant Buddhist ceremony where an individual formally commits to taking solace, or refuge, in three primary things: the Buddha, the goal of enlightenment; the dharma, the teachings which, when practiced, lead to one's achievement of that goal; and the sangha, the community of others who are also on the path toward that goal.

I consider myself a spiritual anarchist, and I appreciate what I can about religions, but I don't like feeling as if I'm subject to their control. "Only with a female rinpoche," I had replied to my fellow retreatants back then, when I was at the retreat and thinking I'd be safe with that decision.

Female rinpoches are not so common, and Khandroma in particular was usually on retreat and therefore unavailable. But that day, high up on a remote Tibetan mountainside, Yongdu was serving as a conduit for me to this legendary female rinpoche. She was the feminine face of a buddha made available to me. Why? Was it because of an off-the-cuff comment I'd made earlier at that retreat, in order to avoid making a religious commitment?

"Okay," I said. It came directly out of my mouth before I could ruminate any further.

I was a bit taken aback at my own acquiescence to the proposal.

On our return hike, I thought out loud, "I mean . . . I don't disagree with Buddhism per se, but I just don't like the patriarchal aspects of it." We resumed our walk over the rocks and grasses.

Short of breath and trying to keep up with Yongdu, I told him I liked what she had said—and, somewhat teasingly, I said, of course I liked her assessment of me. The latter comment got his attention. He looked up at me and smiled as we walked down the grassy slope. "That's an amazing thing to say to you, and I can see why she said it."

THAT EVENING I had some time to think. The idea of "cutting through the ego with a knife" reminded me of one of my favorite chapters in a book by C. S. Lewis called *The Voyage of the Dawn Treader*. In it, an annoying child character named Eustace steals away from the ship he's traveling on with his other childhood companions, and then, while everyone is asleep, he enters a cave, where he chances upon the treasure spoils of a dragon. He chooses a large gold bangle, places it on his arm, and falls asleep atop the remaining treasure.

When he awakens the next day, he finds he's turned into a dragon, and then his challenges are great because he's become fearsome to his shipmates. Soon thereafter, Eustace learns that the ship has problems, and he realizes that, due to his size and strength, he is able to offer help. He sees that he can be of value to the crew, not as a whiny, spoiled child, but as a useful shipmate. Yet the realities of being a large dragon make him feel that he could never truly be a part of the crew again, and he becomes despondent.

In his most despairing moment of utter isolation, the boy is approached by a powerful lion named Aslan, who uses his claw to slice open the skin of Eustace, the dragon, from stem to stern. Layer by layer, the lion peels off the dragon's skin, and it's the last layer that is the most painful for Eustace. Then Aslan, the lion, cleanses the newly humbled boy, who has just emerged from the layers of his former dragon self.

I've often been curious: Is this the best way to deal with the ego—to peel it off, layer-by-layer? Is this the process of personal evolution—to ask for education, and then to awaken the next day and find that one has become a dragon? Is it to see externally all that which has been hidden internally? Could that be what navigating a bardo or period of tribulation entails? Is my ego being exposed, peeled away, stripped, layer by layer, from the last bits, the innermost things I cling to, those that are the most painful to release?

The next day we went to Khandroma Rinpoche's home for the refuge ceremony. Two female friends who wanted to observe and another woman, who also wanted to take refuge, joined me. As we walked up to Rinpoche's cottage, I realized that I had been there before. On a prior trip to Terdrom, even though I did not meet Rinpoche then, as she was sequestered in retreat, I met a man without a tongue, and he ushered a friend and me into her garden for a chance to experience the magic of the water at her sacred well.

Back then, I didn't know that this was her house, but then here I was, once again walking the labyrinth of time in the very same place, yet at a different time in my life. We walked into the small dwelling, where the walls and ceiling were covered with soot from years of cooking over an open fire. And of course, to complete the dreamlike scene, Khandroma was sitting with a black cat on her lap while she pulled on a long cord that controlled the spin of a very large prayer wheel that dominated the room.

She gestured for us to come in, and we prostrated at her feet. When the one other woman and I took refuge, Khandroma recited some words that we repeated back, cut a small lock of our hair, and then gave us each a Tibetan name. I felt suspended and floating out of time as she gave me my name—Kunsang Chödren, which translates roughly as "wholly excellent teacher of the truth, or dharma."

It's strange for me to think back on this now because I was simply too involved in my immediate struggle to really see how this was an answer to a long-held dream—a dream to be seen and acknowledged by such a presence. Sunlight poured down on my head as we departed. I walked out in my bare feet because I had given Khandroma my boots in gratitude for her blessing. Perhaps that's why, later on, walking barefoot became a part of my life's rituals. It became a special way to give thanks to nature and the Goddess. I feel Her under my feet as I walk.

I RETURNED TO Lhasa not long after and had time to spend with Tashi then. Her daughter, who had just returned from a trek, generously gave me one of the loveliest gifts I've ever received. It was a fossil of an old nautilus shell, a predecessor to the conch shell, and it came from the base camp of Mt. Everest, or Chomolungma, which means "Great Mother," in Tibetan.

It was the peak that so many felt compelled to climb. I'd heard numerous stories of great feats occurring in her realm, like that of Erik Weihenmayer, who, in 2001, became the only blind person to have ever made it to the summit, and he was also one of some two hundred climbers—out of a total of some four thousand who have made the climb to date—to have made the full ascent without oxygen.

Then there's the story of the Japanese mountaineer Yuichiro Miura, who made the ascent while carrying his skis and then skied down, in 1970. I was grateful that my drive was about accomplishing something internal, and that I didn't feel compelled to experience even more frostbite and harrowing cirumstances with high altitude and ice.

I'd been to Chomolungma's northern base camp many years earlier, during my first trip to Tibet, when I walked through the shale and saw the rock-engraved names of those who did not survive the climb. I stood at the base of the peak, awestruck and inspired by her height, her beauty, and her power, and I made prayers and asked the Great Mother—long before my entreaty to Venus, at Lake Namtso—what I should do with my life. What came back to me, what I felt in my heart and mind, were two distinct themes to work with: women and leadership. Sadly, as I spoke about the experience later, I had shirked it off as a fantasy that came from a narcissistic part of me. It was a classic move for me, to dismiss my intuition—a behavior that I later learned I'd inherited from my ancestors. Eventually, I came to understand it as a defense mechanism from a process of ancestral transmission designed to protect the patriarchy. I was dampening my feminine power.

At that time the Great Mother was "reaching back," one might say—through Tashi's daughter—and giving me a symbol to dispel and replace those old ways with the power of an ancient teaching. Tashi noted that the conch shell is one of the eight auspicious symbols in the Tibetan Buddhist tradition. She had informed me earlier that it is a symbolic implement used ritualistically for many things, including the awakening of practitioners from the sleep of delusion. She said the sound of the conch inspires us to realize our own well-being and the well-being of others. It was a moving gift to me then, for—unbeknownst to her daughter—I realized it was a wake-up call from Chomolungma herself. The conch shell made me aware that the Great Mother seemed to be saying, "Why not listen to your own inner certainty and be at peace with what you really want to do? Wake up to yourself!"

In that "awake" state, I knew that what I wanted to do was save women from further pain.

Like the meander, whose shape at the heart of its design functions as a symbol, or signal, to go inward, this ancient shell had a similar shape, reminiscent of the thirty thousand-year-old iconic spiral depicted in cave paintings. The strength of the feminine is to receive, and, as I was learning on my journey, there is nothing more powerful than receiving the self. The ultimate gift of going inward was my path to that lovely place—empowerment of the feminine.

As I turned the shell over in my hand, its chalky surface crumbled a bit, and I recalled that I had asked for help from Venus, which symbolized a center of feminine divinity. Again here, the Great Mother, the center of the divine feminine of ancient Tibet, offered me the path—inside.

Then it hit me. I understood why the dakinis were poking at me. My ego was staving me off from my own dream so that I didn't look stupid. It was the ultimate spiritual bypass. The Khandroma was trying to help me see this. I could begin to cut through my ego to awaken the dream that's in my heart, my dream to give due regard to the feminine, rather than bypass her or allow my fear to hold her hostage.

Just as in a labyrinth, where the way in is the way out, my hopes, my desires, and my dreams were like planted seeds. Then, despite my ego, the longing for my dream enabled me to see revealing patterns in the chaos of my pain that were reaching out to help, reaching out to give me clues of where to go to realize this dream. In the face of the unknown, in the face of the extreme, I now recognized my dream as not only worthy of attention but as something material: it was real.

If my dreams were to come true, would that mean that I'd merely had an insight into my future?

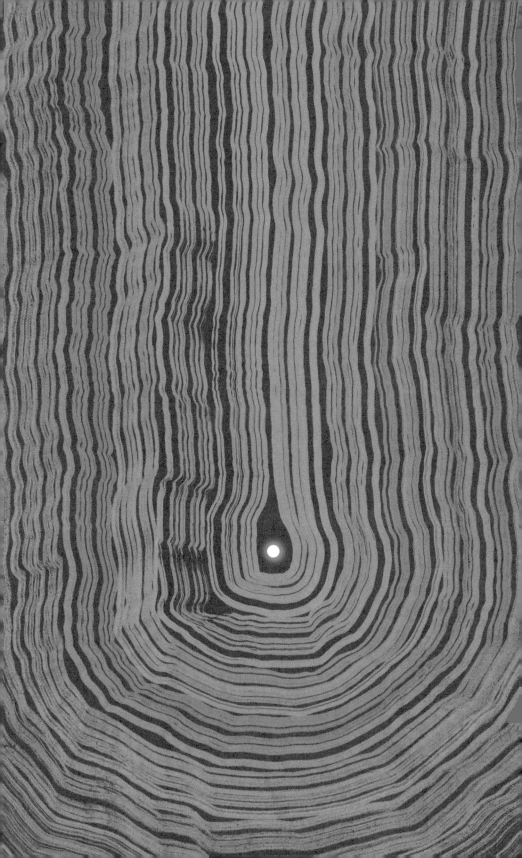

SOLIDARITY

Sorrows are the rags of old clothes and
jackets that serve to cover, then are taken off.
That undressing, and the naked body underneath,
is the sweetness that comes after grief.

RUMI
Translated by COLEMAN BARKS

Despite the magic of Tibet, darkness raged inside me. It felt as though I had received a new sword and magical spells, yet the demons continued to follow me every way I turned.

When my friend Marilyn invited me to her home on a cool November evening, after my mother had divulged to her that my dark night was pitch black, and that I was having difficulty functioning, I went. Years ago, Marilyn had had a crash landing of a similar nature herself, when her whole world broke apart, and I was looking forward to exchanging notes with her, given our similar experiences and the fact that she was steeped in feminism and spirituality.

I swear the fairies were laughing at me as I wound my way through the late-autumn mist, "over the river and through the woods," as the Thanksgiving poem says, to her lakeside retreat. I thought about when we'd first met and how long I'd known her.

Lovely memories returned from a time when the sixties were just behind us, and spirituality was that new territory that everyone wanted a taste of. It was the seventies, the decade of new-age experiments related to the concept of family and a smorgasbord of anecdotal ideas about spirit and health. Marilyn and my mother were chums and comrades for adventures in other dimensions. They were quintessential networkers and acted as the engines of social outreach for the Creative Initiative Foundation (CIF). My mother and Marilyn knew how to work the system and how to sell an unsuspecting friend a whole new paradigm that would delight the senses with things such as high-vibration colors and sounds, along with phone trees for good causes.

Later, in the fall of 1979, Marilyn materialized at a place where I was working during my high school years for a lovely and determined teacher named Joel Rosenberg. I was helping him recruit for his "Communication Skills" workshops for kids my age—teenagers. Marilyn was wearing blue and purple clothing and carried a busy-looking business card. She was in her early forties at the time, and had lots of sparkle and a desire to connect the whole world to that which delighted her. Her spirited enthusiasm was infectious, like a good laugh, and we began a dialogue then that continues to this day. Marilyn reveled in my spiritual longing, took me into the fold of her adventure, and, like Peter Pan and Wendy, we left CIF behind, along with my mother and all of those "poor samsaric slouches," who just didn't understand all the magic that awaited us just behind the curtain.

I learned something really significant at a new-age workshop with Marilyn a number of months later. The idea that everything is related to thought, and that I could create anything was perhaps a bit dangerous at the time. At the end, when I was reborn, in a sense, and felt that workshop-ending intoxication, Marilyn smiled at me but later revealed that she had secretly worried about my innocence and my state as I returned to CIF. She predicted that the naked hot-tub parties and new ideas—such as the concept of "right and wrong" really being an illusion, as we'd learned in this new-age work—would not go over well with the leadership at CIF.

Marilyn also told me stories of "ascended masters," and my mind wandered to thoughts of mystical realms and of devoting my life to spiritual studies. But it wouldn't happen yet because a firmer grounding in my life needed to come about first.

My closest friend called me back into the more conservative folds of my upbringing, and I left the path of purple amethyst crystals and mantras and would not return to Marilyn's world for a good fifteen years.

Marilyn herself left CIF after having a confrontation with CIF's leader that revealed to her the misogynistic and homophobic shadows existing then in parts of the organization, which, like all organizations, even the greatest, had blind spots. In confidence, Marilyn had revealed to her that she thought she might be gay, and the leader, who seemed compassionate about it at the time, went to the larger group and publicly said to Marilyn, "You are the walking, living devil. Now, say it!"

Having been so horribly emotionally hit by the woman she had trusted spiritually, Marilyn left the world she had adored and moved on. Years later, when the politics had changed and the spiritual leader was in an open place, Marilyn, unlike others, invited the leader to her home so they could talk at length about the past, in an attempt to absorb and perhaps heal the experience. That was what was unique about Marilyn: she left no rock unturned.

"Joan and I invited her up," Marilyn later related to me, and said she had told Joan, "You must first tell her that I am with a woman." Joan was the friend who was driving this leader to Marilyn's home. After they'd begun the drive from the Bay Area, Joan told her, and the leader's response was, "Has she forgiven me?" The meeting went fairly well, as Marilyn tells it. That was what was unique about this leader and a testament to the spiritual work in CIF, to face your shortcomings and resolve relationship conflicts. I was proud of both of them.

Marilyn had sought refuge among the Sierra Nevada foothills, where she pursued a life steeped in the divine feminine. It was in her new home with her loving, fabulous partner, Georgia, where she could heal as they surrounded themselves in the beauty of nature and the softness of the feminine.

NOW, FIFTEEN YEARS since I'd had significant contact, and with the grace of the fairies, I "landed" and stepped out of my gold-colored Honda onto her gravel driveway. Marilyn came down and dispensed a motherly hug. She introduced me to Georgia—a spectacularly beautiful woman who immediately felt startlingly familiar. She was an incarnation of Marilyn's exquisite taste. The air was clear and cool, and there was a welcome silence all around.

As I made my way up the stairs, my backpack in tow, I glanced at my surroundings and noted how I loved the way Marilyn used her money to collect large spiritual objects. They helped to anchor the house and grounds in a comfortable vibratory pitch. The memories of my old amethyst adventures worked their way into my parched soul, and that aching feeling of being a sort of alien in the world began to recede during this lovely, fleeting weekend moment, a brief respite from the dark.

They showed me to a cozy room, where I quickly settled in under a quilt, reflected a bit on the drive, and then fell right into a deep sleep. The next day, I awoke refreshed. They'd given me Georgia's healing room—a room surrounded by a range of laminated charts of human anatomy and the physiology of blood vessels and an array of crystals. As I brushed my teeth, I noticed large, glistening stones in the bathroom.

Then I pulled on my sweater and entered the main living area, where I found the two women waiting for me with tea and makings for oatmeal, a fortification for our chat ahead.

Their faces were so receptive that I found myself unleashing everything going on in my mind, and it spread right onto the literal and metaphorical kitchen table. It was evident to me that everything I said—every thought and emotion I expressed—was of interest to them. They wanted to know, and I wanted to tell.

In my professional training, I had worked with trauma, and I knew that the client's retelling of a traumatic event was key to the therapeutic process. Here, these two receptive women were my witnesses, and they listened and listened and listened more, without assigning any judgment or giving advice, to the truth that I was gathering and recounting. It was a gift that women often give—something I now consider to be a sign of direct link to the goddess. We are relational beings, and we know that the "evolution of the soul," as some call it, comes from interaction with the hearts of others.

"I am so tired of people saying, 'you just need to forgive him.' The issue isn't about forgiveness; the issue is about how to recover from the shock. Don't you think it's strange when people say you should forgive someone when there was no forgiveness requested and no apology?" I looked up at them with hope of affirmation.

"You have to be the good girl," Marilyn said to me, sipping her coffee as Georgia kept looking at me, both of them wrapped up in what I was saying. Marilyn's simple seven-word sentence fed me just what I needed. Understanding.

"What I am getting is that women are always supposed to be the better person, and that means taking all of the blame," I said. "I am the one who's shunned as 'the problem' while he was the one having the affairs. He walked away with the house, for god's sake." I could feel the pressure in my temples as my restrained tears of pain began to move to the corners of my eyes.

Georgia poured us more tea. "My dear, you have really been through it," she said. She was so elegantly earnest. Her sparkling eyes danced, and a small chunk of the morning light coming through the window reflected on her shiny jewelry.

"We both know the good-girl routine. Georgia was raised like your mother. She was a debutante from a blue-blood family," Marilyn said.

"Ah yes, the world of thank-you notes, poolside conversations, alcohol, and proclamations about tennis and conservative politics," I said as I took Georgia in. She was a lesbian woman, living in the mountains, and was the perfect paradox for the patriarchy to chew on.

"Yes," Georgia confirmed. "You got it."

She beamed with self-confidence. Her rosy cheeks were a clear sign of health, and her short grey hair had a sort of halo effect on her energetic countenance. Georgia had cut her hair extremely short, she said, "to be in solidarity" with her beloved friend who was in the middle of chemo at the time, and she retained the well-shorn look, even after her friend's death. And, without much hair, Georgia still looked radiant. She was so beautiful and so feminine yet bore none of the prescriptive demands the patriarchal culture held women to regarding wardrobe, hairstyle, lifestyle, or age.

"You must have had to do a great deal of work to be able to come out as a gay woman with your blue-blood pedigree," I said. "How did that go for you?"

She seemed intrigued by my empathy and talked a bit about those challenges. For so long, her pain came from feeling she had to try to be something she was not, she said.

"I left and then found a way of living that was more me. I was raised and trained to relate in an accommodating, hostess-like manner, but deep down, that's not how I like to spend my time," she said.

"You are an introvert, of course!"

"Thank you. Yes."

Georgia turned to me and smiled, seemingly delighted at my description of her nature.

"Unlike me," Marilyn laughed, and we both joined in.

"Marilyn, you make even me look like an introvert," I said. They laughed, and I realized Marilyn's voice was still as astonishingly youthful as it had always been. It reminded me of the clear and cheerful sound of bells.

"You know, as a teenager I was convinced that I knew it all," I said, steering the conversation back to me and getting a laugh from both of them again. "I guess that's not unusual. But I *was* well versed then in the socio-political realities of being a woman. And you and my mother made sure of that with the women's conferences we took part in, not to mention the marches. Do you remember those?"

"How can I forget? We all dressed up in different colors of the rainbow on several occasions, back when that meant forward thinking and a symbol of peace."

I turned to Georgia. "I have to say they were amazing! What I now find interesting is that I knew back then that unequal pay, sexual harassment, and the near-total lack of women in power positions were the prevailing norm . . ."

"Despite overwhelming research concluding that women are highly effective, powerful leaders," Marilyn chimed in.

"Of course," I smiled. "I knew that our mass media allowed for blatant displays of sexism on TV and in movies. And I also knew that unspeakable horrors and crimes were continually being committed against women overseas and even here, merely because we were women.

"It was a cause that I was willing to fight for back then, but a cause that I'd only known intellectually—with the exception of having been a disheartened witness to my father's often demeaning treatment of my mother."

"That's right. I remember, he was verbally tough on your mom," Marilyn said. "He interrupted her all the time—she could never say anything right. Tough."

"Wasn't he? And still is, to a certain extent."

Marilyn nodded in agreement.

"I keep thinking of Charles, when he came to the United States," I said.

"That's her African brother, from Kenya," Marilyn whispered to Georgia.

"I mean, I thought I understood it then, but now that I am more awake, I see that racism and sexism are truly everywhere, you know?"

"Mmm hmm," Georgia uttered with an affirmative nod.

"He experienced blatant racism upon arrival here in the seventies, but even after moving to Northern California, he still had to deal with increasingly subtler forms of racism," I said.

"Comments. Assumptions. I watched him have to continually deal with others' reactions—whether they were conscious of them or not. Yet, he was so calm. How did he do that? How do we deal with it all? My mother tried everything to get my father to change. I tried everything. We were not calm. Now, it's even worse for me. It's hard not to scream. The sexism now seems so bad I wonder if I just didn't see it before, or is it getting worse?"

"Good question," Georgia said supportively.

"It's so weakening . . . I'm not sure that's the right word. Disempowering!"

"Yes. Yes!" Marilyn said and then offered some advice that has stayed with me to this day. "It is everywhere. It's hard to say anything. I've found that in order to gain strength in the truth, one must find others who are willing to speak the truth and be with them."

Georgia put a hand on Marilyn's shoulder. "Marilyn is so talented in building networks, as you know, and she has built an amazing one here too."

"We have built a network," Marilyn said as she turned and looked at Georgia with a proud correction. "We keep each other awake . . . and, you know we have to, so we can wake up the world."

"And remind each other. Yes. Remind each other that the emperor is not wearing any clothes. Yes!" I said. A moment of silence followed, punctuated by the sound of kitchen appliances. "But what I didn't get then," I said, breaking the quiet, "was how the big enemies are right here under my nose. Right in my own bed and now in my social life. It's not out there somewhere."

"That's the hardest thing to get, isn't it?" Marilyn said. "And to explain to others as well."

"It's weird because now that I have been through this I am meeting all of these other women who have been through it far worse than I have. It feels like a Dickens novel—a place where black, soot-covered faces speak about what is real, while the rest of the world sleeps in ignorance and denial, like the aristocracy ignores the plight of the poor. Down in that dark place, I meet women who were not only left just as I was, but women who were nearly fatally beaten. It's an odyssey. I continue to hear the never-ending stories about married men who pursue women while lying and insisting that they're single, and men who date multiple women simultaneously while promising each of them a life of monogamous partnership.

It's not uncommon for a woman to discover that her husband has an entire second family that lives—in some cases—just around the corner. Women in these situations don't talk, unless perhaps their children are at stake, because their stories are often disbelieved, dismissed as hysterical, or their vulnerability appears to others to be a sign of weakness. We're all painfully aware that in order to maintain the illusion, we must submerge the facts. Everyone here is asleep in the patriarchal dream—uh, nightmare, actually! It's sooo frustrating! No one seems to get it. Not to mention that dating is horrible too. I had no idea how bad it would be, and I was so looking forward to it."

"Sounds horrible," Georgia said. "Can you say more?" I loved the way Georgia was so empathetic and curious at the same time. It was such a relief.

"Well, each guy starts off as nice and then quickly becomes a soul-sucking zombie by lying, cheating, or insulting my intelligence."

"Oh, honey."

"It sounds too harsh but it is so real. And when I complain about that to others, do you know what they say?"

"What?"

I lowered my voice to a whisper. *"Boys will be boys! . . . That's just what men do!"* I said, emphasizing every word.

"People have said that to you?"

"Right?" I said, practically falling off of my seat at that point. "I want to yell back at them! I want to say, Is *this* what you tell your daughters?"

They laughed, albeit grimly. I moved back from the edge of the cushion, relaxing into the chair.

I saw their faces, caring and kind, and I softened, adding, "I would do anything for a good relationship." My voice trailed off. The grief and despair closed in on me again, and I started to see a grim future for myself, alone.

"We know, dear," Marilyn said.

The sound of her voice brought me back to my body. With Georgia at her side, she leaned across the table and looked directly at me. "Your mother tells us you've been really depressed, and she's quite worried about you."

"I know," I said.

"Are you okay?" she asked.

"You mean, am I going to hurt myself?"

"Well . . . "

"Honestly, I don't think my mother thinks I'd hurt myself. It's really the crying that's getting to her. Some mornings I just can't stop. Intuitively, I know that hurting myself wouldn't have any effect. Wherever I go, here I am." I said, breaking the tension.

They both laughed.

"Well, I agree, and I'm relieved." Marilyn said, finally.

"I came nose to nose with the concept of dying and with having some capacity to end it all when I was sick with a feverish dysentery, in a bathroom in Pokhara, Nepal," I said.

"We've been there. It's so beautiful," Marilyn said. "But dysentery? In a bathroom in Nepal? Is that as wretched is it sounds?"

"Yes, not a good place to die," I said.

"My boyfriend had just broken up with me; according to him, he now needed to be celibate. However, as I lay in my room with this horrible fever, I could hear him having sex with the woman staying in the next room."

"You've got to be kidding! After all you'd been through!" they exclaimed.

"I'd been fainting again and again while trying to reach the bathroom down a long hallway, with my head aching so much that I started to wonder if my anger combined with my fever might cause all of my synapses to simply burn out. I imagined how the electricity in my brain would simply cease and then I'd start to decay. All of the things that were stored in my brain and in my body—all of the songs I knew, the capacity to understand poetry, my relationships, all of the beauty I'd experienced in my life; if I were to die, all of that would be gone. I considered it for a moment. Was I really ready to let all of that disappear? And then I realized I didn't want to die alone in a bathroom in Nepal."

Marilyn exhaled.

"So I closed my eyes and imagined, as clearly as I could, this lovely Welsh woman who had commiserated with me the day before and who was staying in a room nearby. When I opened my eyes I saw her actually standing, like a miracle, right there before me. She wrapped my arm around her neck, propped me up, and then dragged me back to my room and found help."

"Fabulous," Georgia said. "She just appeared."

"Now . . . my mother is encouraging me to get some psychotropic meds, and I keep telling her that I just don't want that. I've worked with people on those kinds of meds, and it's not the way I want to handle my situation now. I do understand that she wants me out of pain. I want out of pain. But meds just aren't the way to go, for me.

"As luck would have it, though, I became connected with this renowned female therapist who'd been through something really similar to my experience."

"Of course you were," Georgia giggled.

I laughed with her, knowing what she meant. Despite all of my pain, I managed to meet extraordinary people along the way, just as Psyche had done.

"This therapist's divorce tale was quite painful," I went on, "and she had also come through a prolonged and deep dark night. I'll never forget what she told me: 'After all of my training and experience, I knew I needed to feel everything in order to move through it.' She said she absolutely didn't want to be anesthetized then because she said she knew, in order to really heal, she'd want to feel every aspect of her experience, so that she wouldn't have to repeat it."

"She sounds courageous," Georgia said.

"You know, this was really one of the first pieces of advice that made sense to me.

"And I realized that people who have walked down a similar road—especially an emotionally draining one—have a less anxious investment in getting you out of your pain," I said.

"Yes." Georgia chimed in. "That is the reality. Those who've been there know it is something more precious and something to process."

"It seems like they have more compassion and acceptance of your pain."

"And are often a solid hand to help," Marilyn added.

"Yes, and you'll never believe it . . . she and her ex-husband are remarried now."

"Ummm."

"And you know what?"

"What?"

"In the burned-out caverns of my grief, hearing her say 'back together' struck me like a love story that I would've wanted to tell too."

"I hope this doesn't mean you want to get back together with Chuck," Marilyn said.

"Hell, no!" I said.

"Whew!" they said, in unison.

"Someone once told me—and I'm not sure who it was or if what this person said is medically advisable, but it made sense to me—that if you heal an infection without an antibiotic, your body will gain more ability, or strength, to fight future infections. Now, I wouldn't attempt to do that today, with or without antibiotics, without consulting a physician first because infections are very tricky. But the analogy is what interests me."

"That is interesting," Marilyn said.

"I think that, in a way, this is the same approach that the therapist had taken with her own emotional work."

"That makes sense."

"And so," I said, "I've made a similar decision."

"Meaning?"

"Instead of taking meds, I've also decided to allow myself to feel everything, so that I don't have to repeat it again. I want my body to learn to take care of itself."

"You want to evolve through the pain."

"Exactly—" I said, "as opposed to insulating myself from it."

"You might have been too young, Sus," Marilyn said, "but this conversation reminds me of when Valium addiction was epidemic during the sixties and seventies."

"Yes!" I said, sitting up. "I talk about this in my class. It was primarily male doctors then who were so liberally prescribing Valium to their female patients who suffered depression."

"That's right."

"It's a way of keeping women asleep to the humiliation they endure," I said.

"Instead of staying asleep, you're taking back the reins of your own personal power. That's hard to do, Susie," Georgia said. "Perhaps one of the hardest things a person can do. And you are doing it."

"It's painful to stay awake," I said.

I looked up at them and knew that my lantern for this sunless land would have to be continued blind faith in the practice of lucid living—a faith that the ensuing adventure done *awake* would lead me toward healing.

Marilyn and Georgia agreed.

AS I BEHELD these two beautiful women and the compassionate expressions on their faces, I felt grace.

Their solidarity reminded me of a time when I participated in a nude peace march down a main thoroughfare in San Francisco. I glanced over at a friend I was demonstrating with and noticed she'd kept her pearls on. They were luminous against the dark nighttime, so raw, so natural, fashioned by the repeated polishing of an unwanted irritant.

The pearls she'd left on her otherwise naked body were the unmistakable bright essence that endures when there's nothing else. Both the polishing of the pearls and the processing of our pain as women were "irritants" now made beautiful—adornments of the soul.

I became grateful for my body, grateful to be alive, and grateful to begin to hold the pearl that symbolized my newfound perspective, a pearl fashioned from those tough experiences that have helped me to now become a better person.

That night, naked and marching on the city street, we were vulnerable and exposed to the elements, like new life, or an idea taking form.

Now I understand why, in Nathaniel Hawthorne's *Scarlet Letter*, the protagonist—who was publicly punished, shamed, and imprisoned for bearing an illegitimate child in a Puritan village—named her baby Pearl. Like her tribulations, my own emotional pain was waking me up to the truth. In solidarity with these strong women on the peace march, we were creating an iridescent light around our sad reality, to transform it into divine experience.

"I have a little something for you," Georgia said, taking my hand. She walked me into the living room.

A sea of colors—turquoise, cobalt, and violet—washed over me. A song by the Indigo Girls infused the room: "Fugitive," a favorite of mine. With the vivid poetry of the words, I became conscious that I had a fugitive, ancient and now reborn, embryonic, and forming itself inside my solar plexus. This fugitive was my absconder from the lies. She was my witness to the truth. She was pure expression. Now that I was aware of her, feeling her heartbeat in rhythm with mine, all I wanted to do was keep her alive, to protect her at all costs. I started moving with the music as the stirring lyrics of the chorus made her purpose more palpable. I felt like there was actual sand beneath my feet, and I was naked to the elements of the world. There was nothing left to protect because I walked with the shamed and the damned, self-governing and free.

HEART OF THE MATTER

*A thousand half-loves must be forsaken
to take one whole heart home.*

RUMI
Translated by COLEMAN BARKS

BLACK BOX

The walls of my office, perched above The Roastery, were embedded with the smell of coffee and sweet vanilla. That, plus the muffled sounds from creaky stairs, ringing telephones, and sundry street noise gave my space a cheerful, classic, city feel, a place where the past, present, and future met.

On this particular day, the next client on my schedule, a woman in her twenties, had just entered my treatment room and taken her seat on the blue denim couch. Then she told me the story of her sad childhood. She was extremely intelligent, and she'd come from an impoverished background where she found herself situated in a juxtaposition of divided worlds that composed her life.

She picked up a thin black pen and drew a caricature of herself on an island. I watched her pull the pen across the page. For weeks she'd been drawing images of herself trapped behind walls and pushing against them.

"Did you know," she said while she drew, as though in a trance, "that I am terrified of black holes?"

"I didn't know that. Why are you terrified of black holes?"

"Because," she said, as she lay down her pen and looked at me, "black holes are structures in space where not even light can escape. Darkness overcomes everything and sucks you in. It's almost the opposite of matter, I believe. Nothing can exist."

It was dark when I left my office. I eased into my car, briefcase and coat in hand, and drove north across the Golden Gate Bridge, heading home. The fog was uncharacteristically thick for that time of year, and the temperature was cold. The darkness and reduced visibility alerted me to be extra cautious with driving, and my thoughts about that last session began to accelerate.

She was afraid of black holes? Sucks you in to . . . nothing? Is it a fear of nonexistence, or something else? A fear of extinction? Suddenly, the image of an atom floated in my mind. I turned it around, as though receiving just the right clue at the right moment—how does that happen so often?

I remembered that an atom is mainly composed of nothing but empty space—one might say "nothingness." Electrons determine the pattern of matter, but they, and the protons at their center, are so minuscule that, in proportion to the space they hold, they make the atom a container of practically nothing. The odd aspect that I remembered from basic physics is that electrons appear as probability patterns until you look for them, or something like that. To me, the most mysterious element in the atom is this almost-complete emptiness. Interesting, I thought. Does she fear this nothingness, emptiness, or void—the opposite and yet essential aspect of matter? Is this "empty" pattern of the atom some kind of "perceived magnification in form" of our existential predicament—what we humans all feel and suffer, in varying degrees, to come to terms with? Is it somehow a projection of the mind?

As if on cue not too many days after that, another client arrived in my office and shared a similar sensation about being behind walls. She was fifteen. She had hit her sister and was consequently required to see me. She drew herself stuck inside a rectangular black box.

"Can you tell me what is happening outside that black box?" I said.

In a very cool tone, she said, "People are walking by me, but, unlike me, they can do whatever they want."

She rolled her eyes, and I imagined high school and the feeling of everyone else having it better than oneself.

"If you look at the walls of the box, what are they made of?"

"Fabric."

"And if you were to zoom in on the fabric, and see it as if it were under a microscope, what would you see *it's* made of?"

She quickly reached for her pen and drew repeated patterns across the page again and again.

"The wall is made of something that looks like snowflakes."

I caught my breath. She was drawing mandalas.

Mandalas are universal designs that symbolize all of creation. Both of these clients were revealing something that many other clients had also shared in different yet parallel ways. Was it possible that they were connecting with a truth beyond themselves, a truth about the collective human experience that is shared at a universal level? On an unconscious level, do we all experience being behind walls? Being on islands? Being separate from others? What was this about? Why were they having these visions, and, most important, how does one "remove" the wall?

A CLUE ARRIVED a few days later at my fractal geometry discussion group. We met in a friend's living room. She had a little apartment facing the ocean, where we could hear the waves.

"By any chance, does anyone here know anything about black boxes?" I said. "I have a client who drew herself inside a black box. What could that mean?"

"Do you know about the black cube?" someone said.

"I don't," I said. "What is that?" *I knew I'd come to the right place.*

"We each have a black cube around our third eye," he said as he gently placed his index finger between and a little above his eyes.

"It looks like this," he said, and reached for an oversized, heavy-looking white book, which he opened and spread across his lap while he sat crosslegged and flipped through the pages, to an image of a black cube. Then he drew a woman's face, with a shiny black box hovering right between her closed eyes. The image caught me. I could hear the sounds of the ocean waves, and I dropped into some place out of time.

"It's related to the Kabbalistic cube."

"What is that?" I asked.

"It symbolizes the process of cubing space," he said.

"But why cube space?" I asked.

"We cube things to understand them. We cube our reality so we can observe it. It's our way of concretizing things. In our attempts to understand things, we box them in."

"Kind of like a square Petri dish?"

"You could say that. Eventually, if we aren't careful, we believe the cube *is* reality. That reality ends where we cube it. If we realize that the only reason we cubed space in the first place was to understand it, not to contain it, then we can work our way out of these limitations. This is a helpful process if we get to that place where the cube becomes confining and no longer works."

The topic was a hot one, and there were many ideas flying back and forth. I heard at one point about the Jewish ceremony that includes removing the cube from the forehead. Towards the end of our group's time together, my phone began to vibrate in my pocket.

"Hey, babe," I said to my boyfriend as I answered my red flip phone.

"We have to go see this movie! We *have* to go see this movie!" he said. "It's called *The Hurricane*."

His insistence caught me by surprise. But I was in Santa Cruz. And I didn't really want to see a movie then.

"Really? I still have to drive over the hill," I said with discernible fatigue in my voice.

"I know," he said hurriedly, which meant he was like a dog with a bone, and he wasn't going to relent. "You have time to get here, no problem."

"Ok, I'll leave in ten," I said with reluctance. His persistence always hooked me, and I found it was easier to cave-in than fight his latest fascination. I drove over the steep curves of Highway 17, which I'd always found unnerving, and, oddly enough, I arrived at the theater in plenty of time and met him outside. When we stepped into the theater lobby, we were greeted by the familiar sounds of kids' arcade games. We located the right screening room and cocooned ourselves in large velvet chairs and waited for the previews.

I was digesting this new information about the black cube, and I kept chewing on the question: how do we get out of the black box if we are stuck in it? If I could answer this, I could help my clients get out of these stuck places, these metaphorical boxes, too.

"Do you know what the movie is about?" my boyfriend mumbled through a mouthful of popcorn.

I wondered if I'd been speaking my musings out loud. "No, I don't have any idea," I replied.

"The movie is about a boxer named Hurricane Carter. It's about his life and how he got out of prison. I thought you'd love it. It's with Denzel Washington."

Was I hearing him correctly? A black boxer? A black man in a box?

The lights dimmed. The projector clicked. And the story unfolded.

An African-American man, a boxer, is in prison and wants to get out. In many different ways he attempts to do so, and nothing works. Eventually, with no other option remaining, Rubin "Hurricane" Carter retreats inside himself and writes his autobiography. One day, a kid originally from Brooklyn picks it up, reads it, and falls totally in love with this story of Hurricane, who is still languishing in prison.

So this young boy, Lesra, goes to meet the author—in prison—and this boxer-turned-author, Rubin Carter, and he become friends. In fact, they become so close that eventually Lesra works very hard to secure Rubin's release. At one point, just before the judge hears the very last appeal, Lesra tells Rubin that he is going to bust him out if the judge rules against his appeal. His fierce display of solidarity in this desperate moment was raw and pivotal to their story. It was *the* black box. Lesra displayed that youthful part in all of us that could feel the edges of the box not as a final prison but as a cocoon. It was something to burst out of—transformed, regardless of its former limitations.

It was then that Rubin looked at his young friend, and, with a gentle laugh, answered my own inner query. "Hate put me in prison; love's gonna bust me out," he said.

It was the answer I was looking for. Getting out of the box had something to do with love.

Suddenly, a door opened in my mind, and immediately it all made sense. In my apperception, I saw myself *inside* the black box. Its walls were immeasurably high. I felt the dark, plush softness of the theatre surrounding me. Screens were everywhere, and in the center of the black box, a projector threw images onto every wall. I imagined touching the walls, and they were merely images, like mirrors. I stepped toward the center. Red, red, red. It was alive at the center. As I looked closer, I realized what the aliveness was. It was beating, and oh my god, it was my optical nerve intertwined with my heart. My heart was the optic nerve. My heart was my sight.

"It's through the heart that you can see a way out," said a voice.

"A way out of the box?" I asked. The voice seemed to come from everywhere.

"Love is expansive. It is limitless. Everything is available," I heard the voice say.

"How?"

"Go into the depths of your own heart," the voice replied.

"How do I do that?"

The projector in my inner vision then turned off, and all faded to nothingness.

"In the beginning, God created the heavens and the earth," the voice said. "The earth was formless and void, and darkness was over the surface of the deep, and the Spirit of God was moving over the surface of the waters."

Yes, I thought, the void, emptiness—this is the place, the place that is totally unknown, totally unscripted. Would it suck me in? I had heard of great Buddhist lamas who had contemplated emptiness. I compared my idea of their meditations that went so deeply inward with the idea of going inside the atom.

My client's drawings of snowflakes came to mind, and I realized that the pattern in the snowflakes represented atoms and their electron patterns. She was drawing space as the substance of the material, which was what the cube was made of: the electron patterns of an atom, and the space in between.

"The optical nerve is the genesis of all life," the voice said. "How life appears is how life is."

I heard my heartbeat. I realized that the projector was back on—and I *am* the projector; I am the audience; I am the writer. I am not an actor in someone else's play; I am every actor in the story of my life. When I step into that space, I can actually create the life that I want, I can manifest my dream. The projector changes images on the walls because I change. The story manifests because I write the script.

That's why I can't really get out of the walls of the box or change the walls of the box by manipulating anything that appears on the outside, I thought. The projector is inside.

That's when I figured it out.

I have to shift "me." I have to shift my internal seed—so that I can grow a different tree, so that I can manifest the world that I want.

Is that what is meant by the mustard seed of faith? I asked myself.

I can create anything in the space of emptiness, from nothingness?

I realized that I had to shift myself at a very deep level. I knew that if I just changed what was in my head, that wouldn't help. It had to be a full shift. I knew it. I could feel it. I could see glimpses of my life as I wanted it to be. My heart, my brain, my intestines—in all ways, I had to open to that place, that seed, of possibility. I wanted to shift all the centers of intelligence in my body. Everything inside me had to change. As a systems therapist, I knew that if I could shift one part of me, then other parts would also start to shift. I wanted my reality to be about love. I wanted all of reality to be about love, for women—and for men who see women as intelligent and wise.

"How we see life is how life will be," I said to the voice.

But the voice was gone. Or, as I was thinking about it later, I wondered, is it that the voice is perhaps always here, and I *am* the voice?

My perception of the theater became normal again, the movie finished, and we left for home. It was not long until my fortieth birthday, and a friend sent me a birthday card in a teal envelope. It was a Zen birthday card, and in one simple line it summed up the black-box question—"I'm standing so far inside myself that I'm outside myself."

I began to think that I'd stumbled onto the meaning of samsara—that is, being stuck in life's endless cycle.

Samsara, simply put, can be thought of as the orientation of our mind in regard to wanting or not wanting certain experiences, over and over again, in an unceasing pattern. In our mind, which is like a projector, if the movie of our life is oriented toward constantly desiring pleasure and running away from pain, then we are stuck in a never-ending cycle of dissatisfaction. If, instead, we choose to change the script, to rewrite the play, we can begin to break the cycle of dissatisfaction by acting with compassion, by having positive intent, and by wanting to help and serve others. This loosens our attachment, and every moment that we are at one with others or at one with our self, we are no longer in samsara; we are in nirvana. If hate gets us into this samsaric cycle, love is what gets us out!

It's a release from prison when we shift our entire being toward love. We feel at one—at peace—in our life. To be able to create good screens, or loving projections, for our "self" means that we can create good screens seen by us all. As these thoughts swirled and spiraled around me, a wellspring of hope bubbled up within me, and I felt warm.

Beginner's mind
Practiced heart

GRASPING SELF

No one can make you feel inferior
without your consent.

Attributed to ELEANOR ROOSEVELT

I began to figuratively step away from my life and the projections on the walls of my box. I was trying to determine what the images on the screen of my life were trying to tell me about my own mind—how it all worked. I felt as if I were meeting myself again and again in the corridors of my psyche. I had to look in that mirror all the time, and the painful self-reflections it revealed inspired me to do that very difficult thing—change myself.

As I went inside, I used the feeling of warmth to navigate and serve as my guidepost indicating where I was feeling love. With time, my journey inside became easier and easier. Suddenly "how to" clues popped up everywhere. Perhaps they had been there all along, and I just hadn't noticed them much. Now they were everywhere. Some of the clues came when I was alone, some came while I was standing in random places, and some came in dialogue with others. Still, more clues resurfaced, ones that I resurrected from my years in academia. Some just jumped out at me from quotes and passing comments. Above all, it seemed as if there were a chorus of help that voiced ways for me to source my innermost self—that part of me that was deeply connected to the eternal well of life—the well that is without ego.

One day, during a very simple lunch conversation with a friend, I found that all of this boiled down to one sentence he related to me.

Daniel Kottke was one of the most connected people I'd ever met. He knew everyone, and he was a quirky, kind engineer with his own bardos to deal with. He had been the first employee at Apple, and according to him, Steve Jobs had made sure he walked away from that experience with almost nothing. I sensed that Daniel knew a thing or two about betrayal.

"Why did my ex-husband hate me so much?" I asked him. "I mean, I was picking up his dry cleaning, for crying out loud. What did I do that could create such hate?" I couldn't figure it out.

"He accused me of being suspicious of him, but, oh," I began laughing, "the sweet irony of that."

"How is it that the world favors the strong while it silences victims and the truth?" I questioned out loud.

"I was with Ram Dass last week when a friend of mine who was there complained to him that I'd been betrayed by Steve," Daniel told me, with a look that seemed to suggest that he was going to share something with me that might be of use. "Though *I* would never have said it that way," he added.

"Ram Dass responded with just one thing: 'Betrayal, isn't that all about the ego?'"

"All about the ego," I repeated. "So that means that what gets hurt is the ego?"

"I don't know," Daniel said.

I felt for the small dakini knife emblem on the chain around my neck. Why hadn't I considered this before?

I chewed on remembrances of the usual ego lectures that I gave to my grad students. "I think a dictionary definition would say the ego concerns the self, and maybe it would mention self-esteem as well. Freud believed the ego is an intermediary between the id and the superego. Jung believed the ego is where our conscious awareness is located, a smaller part of the larger Self that includes the unconscious."

"Sounds right," Daniel said.

I felt my solar plexus again and the pain of betrayal lodged there. It came to me in conjunction with Ram Dass's sentence that was lingering with me.

"What if I was asking the wrong question? What if the question is not 'Why was I hurt by my ex-husband?' but rather, '*What* was hurt by my ex-husband?'"

"I think you're on to something," Daniel said.

I repeated Khandroma's sentence aloud: "You can cut through the ego with a knife."

"What?"

"Something a female Rinpoche said once, describing me. I guess the question is that if ego can be cut, then what comprises the ego?"

"That's a good question," he said.

I ARRIVED HOME and was greeted by a grim reflection of myself in the mirror. I had lost weight, and my face was gray and pallid. That scared me. I touched the mirror and imagined it as the wall of my box. Why did it scare me? Because I am getting older, I thought. I'm no longer as beautiful as I once was, and I've always considered my physical beauty a part of my power. Wait. Was the need to be beautiful a part of my own defense? I felt powerful when I looked good, and yet that condition was always going to be fleeting. What else was there that I figured I needed to be? Nice, kind, forgiving?

Was I required to not only be beautiful, but also nice, kind, accommodating, and easygoing? Was this my ego? Was it a compilation of being friendly, kind, pretty, selfless, and eager to help, among many other things? Had I crafted a personality such that I couldn't conceive of someone wanting to hurt me? Was that my ego? Who could betray that? It would be like betraying a kitten. I could almost sense my ego's aliveness, like a jellyfish in my solar plexus. I closed my eyes, and I could see and feel this fabric of threads and nerves that my ego had woven. If someone touched the fabric favorably, as in telling me how deep, pretty, or self-sacrificing I was, I felt relieved. If someone told me the opposite, like I looked old or that I was selfish, it was terrifying to me. Each thread had a sensory signal, a bundle of nerves devised to alert my system when any one of them registered my reaction. Each of these threads was constructed and then woven together with the others by me, a participant in an ancient system.

I imagined living without those ego-driven qualities, and then I felt deeper into the emotions that were present, given that I'm driven by my ego. I noticed that the terror felt to me like the fear of death. I was so afraid of not being seen as beautiful that death actually seemed easier. Yes, not being seen as beautiful was worse than death: for me, a lack of beauty was actually a fear of nonexistence.

If the man with whom I'd pledged to spend my life could so easily betray me, with such readiness, then that meant I was not safe. My kitten-like defenses of beauty, innocence, and appeal were meaningless and ineffective. With this thought, the fabric of my jellyfish-like ego quivered again. While I knew that I could no longer sustain all that my ego wanted, I was still bending to its whims in desperation. I was clinging to these threads for survival. I was clinging to the familiarity of an idea of self that no longer fit. I couldn't change how I appeared in the mirror, yet every time I looked, I hoped that my aging was not really happening.

This is clearly one example of what Buddhists refer to when they talk about clinging. Riches weren't my substance of choice, but what if being seen as selfless, helpful, smart, and, most of all, beautiful were the riches that I sought? The word for ego in Tibetan is *dak dzin*, which can also be translated as "self-grasping."

I was grasping at the past, I was grasping at old, ineffective ways to survive. I was onto something.

Silence the chatter in your head
To hear what your heart has to say.

THE ENEMY

So many people throughout my life have told me who I am, what I must do, what I can't do, what I have to complete, and what I will never be able to accomplish, and then I met the goddess.

AMYTHYST RAINE HATAYAMA

I began having visions again, and they were similar to the ones I had experienced at my divorce proceedings. I found myself walking through underground caverns with pillars and inlaid marble floors. A child and a mummy were with me. I figured this vision was like a dream and also like an exploratory surgery of my psyche; I was taking two aspects of myself into this labyrinth to see how to approach my "self." I figured that the mummy was the aspect of me that was dead and looking for eternal life, and the child was maybe my "beginner's mind."

One day, while at the beach, although I didn't have a vision, I definitely felt kinesthetically compelled to repeatedly draw large spirals in the sand. The fog along the beach seemed so soothing as the waves differentiated themselves from other waves and then merged back again. I could not understand what was arising in me and then manifesting in this urgent need to make spirals, over and over, with a stick in my hand as my feet dug into the cold sand.

Not too long after, I was at a friend's bookstore when a woman named Esperide came in. At the time, Esperide seemed exotic and somewhat distant, a bit like an alien. She was from a community in

Italy called Damanhur, and she told us about this fantastical place that I could hardly believe existed in real life. She said Damanhur is a community outside the northern Italian city of Turin (or Torino, as it's called there), and the centerpiece of that community is known as the Temple of Humankind, which this group of Damanhurians secretly began to construct inside a mountain there, in 1978. Esperide said it was built "to bring spirit into matter."

As she described the temple, with spirals and underground tunnels, I realized that I'd been having visions of Damanhur without even knowing it. The temple was beyond anything I'd ever heard of: a four thousand-square-meter structure (with almost 150,000 cubic feet of earth removed), inside a mountain filled with "spiritual" technology and art.

My friend and I were speechless as we listened to Esperide. At the time of our meeting, the temple and the community were barely public knowledge. My friend wanted to go to Italy to film it, and months later, after he'd obtained permission to do so, he invited me to go with him, and we were off.

NOVEMBER IN NORTHERN Italy was not warm, but the area had a flavor of medieval beauty and a quality of freshness among the trees and mist. Damanuhur itself is a community of about seven hundred people, complete with its own culture, theology, currency, and educational system. Our sleeping arrangements were just as those of the Damanhurians: we stayed in what was called a *nucleo*, a configuration of several families, in a beautiful thousand-year-old farmhouse.

My friend filmed during the daytime, and I explored the temple's elaborate halls and caverns while shooting still-life photographs. Above ground, the grass lawns were decorated with different colors of spiral rock designs. Inside, the temple was filled with marble inlaid floors and terracotta pillars.

I was emotionally triggered as I took it all in because this environment was the same three-dimensional space I'd been envisioning and drawing before I even knew of the temple's existence. I noticed that my breathing was shallow and my body was tense, as if I couldn't handle the excitement.

My eyes feasted on the stained-glass windows and on the doors, domes, and frescos of life that surrounded me everywhere there. I let the environment envelop me as I lay on the floors, sat on the steps, and snapped picture after picture inside this great temple.

The Hall of Earth, one of the rooms in this panoply of color and form, was two, maybe three, stories tall. Every inch, including the Tiffany-style features and terracotta pillars, was covered in frescoes that evoked an otherworldly yet familiar feel. To be so completely surrounded by such an array of collective artistic expression was new to me.

One particular frescoed wall caught my attention. It was a painted section depicting a gathering of people making their way around the foot of a great mountain. Next to the humans were purplish gray beings, painted as if they had bodies of some sort, but their color suggested that they weren't entirely human. They seemed to hover beside the humans, as if they were trying to communicate something to the people they were near. I was struck by the portrayals of those beings. One day, I asked one of my friends in the community who those creatures were.

"They're the enemy."

"Who is the enemy?"

"The enemy is the phenomenon that is always next to us—next to us and always saying, 'You can't.'" She spoke with a deep voice.

"The enemy is a counterforce to creativity. It's the energy that dispels new thought and imagination. We all have the enemy inside us," she answered in a matter-of-fact tone.

I chewed on that for a minute. We were sitting in the Hall of Earth. A sky of frescoes loomed above us showing star formations from a distant past, all illuminated in these vast caverns by the artificial lights carefully placed throughout. The rhythm of her story was slow and sweet, and her voice was laced with a pleasant Italian accent.

"There once was a man who faced the enemy. In our tradition, this is the story of a hero's journey, and it comes to us from a time before Atlantis. The main character is Anansel, a prince who embarks on a journey to find his values and his role for his people. He passes many tests, and eventually he encounters the enemy."

To hear her share this amidst the astonishing view of colors, patterns, and lights was like being in a dream. I couldn't believe I was there, in a real yet fantasy-like temple inside a mountain, in a community where people shared poetic stories from myths I'd never heard. I felt as if I were in a magical book from childhood.

"The enemy tells Anansel how inferior he is because he is human, weak, and stupid. 'I am superior to you! You are inferior to me!' the enemy proclaims. 'You are weak!' The hero of the story says, 'Yes, yes, I am! And it is in my weakness that I will destroy you.'"

"Brilliant," I said to my new female friend, and she flashed a smile that would launch a few ships. To me, she really looked the part of a temple goddess-priestess.

This simple aphorism made my dream real. Anansel was now my hero because what the enemy had called in him a weakness had brought him no shame. He could not be humiliated if he saw power in his own weakest link. This Damanhurian story had resurrected a deep truth. I saw that if I could come to accept my weakest link, the most vulnerable aspects of myself, then I would be free of the enemy, too.

But the real bake-my-noodle truth was that something so primordial could be embraced through that so-called "flaw."

As I thought about my ex-husband and all the unskillful men I was unconsciously drawing to me, I began to think, what did they have in common? What were they saying to me? They seemed to be saying, in a chorus, "You're less than! You're weak!" And what if I'd then said, "Okay, I will step into that weakness and be who I am. That which you judge in me I will wear on my sleeve"?

The way was becoming clearer: I can face my own enemy by being who I am and by being willing to be flawed, to make mistakes—to make mistakes until what emerges is that which I, uniquely, can offer the world.

People who go about seeking to change the world,
to diminish suffering, to demonstrate any kind
of enlightenment, are often as flawed as anyone else.
Sometimes more so. But it is the awareness of having
faults, I think, and the knowledge that this links
us to everyone on Earth, that opens us to
courage and compassion.

ALICE WALKER

THE PROJECTOR

*The most potent weapon in the hands of the
oppressor is the mind of the oppressed.*

STEVEN BIKO

My girlfriend Andrea and I always went to Dinah's Poolside Café, a great little motel with a café adjacent to a swimming pool. It had a huge sculpture of an elephant and a koi pond, which, strangely enough, didn't conflict with the minimalist sixties-style architecture of the building. For me, it was an old haunt rediscovered; I just liked the place.

One Saturday, Andrea and I met there to commiserate. It had been two years since I'd had my vision in the courtroom, and by then I'd managed to get into another relationship that had ended in a way that was similar to the ending of my marriage. I was bone-weary of this habit, and I wanted a change.

When Andrea arrived, I gave her a big hug and watched her as she maneuvered herself into a seat at our small wooden table that offered a direct view of the pool.

Just a week prior, Andrea was with me when my now-ex-boyfriend had called my cell phone, angry and wanting to speak to me. Out of obligation, I had felt that I should answer, but Andrea could see that I didn't want to. Just a day before the call, I had discovered he was cheating, and I had left our home with all my belongings, while he was away.

So she answered the phone for me because Andrea is one of those kinds of friends, and she knew that I was far too vulnerable in that moment to be practical. I watched her listen to him on the other end of the line.

"Ahhh. Uh-huh. I see, you really want to talk to Susie."

She shot me a glance.

"Okay," she told him, slowly handing the phone to me. But mid-pass, she dramatically pretended to slip, and she "accidentally" hung up the phone and giggled.

"Whoops!"

NOW HERE WE were a week later, two women of kindred spirit, sitting at this Palo Alto institution. Andrea is also a therapist, and I knew she could help me piece together all of these insights.

"Everything has been sort of happening all at once," I told her.

"There are clues everywhere—that movie about the boxer and the black box, the chat with Daniel about ego, my dakini knife, betrayal, and now Damanhur and the enemy. I want to know how, as women, we get ourselves stuck in these patterns, how *I* have gotten stuck in these patterns of relationship.

"Are you up for an experiment?" I said.

"You bet, babe," she said.

I was warmed by the pure love of solidarity I felt for her in joining with me.

"I can't seem to understand these experiences. They're coming up like a recurring nightmare. These patterns, I believe, are reflecting something unskillful inside me. I need to find that, and I need to talk to that part of me."

"Unskillful?" she said.

"Something inside me, and I don't know what it is, whether it's what I am thinking, or whether I'm haunted, or what. But something inside me is attracting negativity. In my life, the clues seem to appear in my interactions with men."

"Let's do this after we order," she said.

I watched her pick up her menu and I could see her French-manicured nails. Like Georgia, she did not fit the patriarchal ideal. She too was flat-out gorgeous—she sparkled and would have given even Aphrodite a run for her money; however, her crime against fashion was not voluntary. She was several sizes "too large."

I felt comforted by my friend sitting right before me, who was willing to walk the "caverns of dread" with me.

"And the scariest thing is that—given the repetition, the similarities—I can't deny my realization that I am contributing to this in some way," I said as I settled back into my chair a little, after we'd ordered our food.

"Yuck, yuck, yuck," Andrea said, grimacing.

"I thought this habit of mine had ended—but now, I wonder. Does that mean the closer I get to the truth, the more difficult life will become?

"I'm so sick of this—even though it's absurd, it still impacts me—but I am so done with these problems. I am done with the shame," I said.

I moved my legs out from under the table. I'm tall, and restaurant tables are never high enough for me to comfortably cross my legs beneath them.

"Chuck got everything—the house, a new life, and now a new marriage. I feel like I'm living in a B movie."

"You *know* that I know," Andrea said.

She smiled and giggled lovingly at the absurdity of it all. She had experienced her share of it, perhaps even more than I had.

I leaned forward, toward her, smiling as well.

"I do know I want to change this. I am so ready. The challenge is this: how do I directly engage this stuff? Why is it not so apparent, yet so painful?"

I paused.

"It's weird, isn't it? You and I are extensively educated in helping others, but we can't seem to help ourselves," I said.

"You can say that again. I keep working and working on myself, and I'm not getting anywhere with this either."

Piles of French toast arrived with butter and pure maple syrup. I was slicing up the strawberries as she leaned forward with a whimsical expression. She tilted her head at an ever-so-slight angle.

"We've faced ghosts and abusive men together, but, as you would say, 'This is just another dragon,'" she said.

"Okay, are you up for trying something?" I was inspired, and as I spoke, I could feel my eyes straining, as if I were a goldfish trying to escape a bowl by staring plaintively at the distorted, blurry object moving beyond the glass.

Andrea confirmed her characteristic full loyalty, saying, "I'm in. What do you want to do?"

"Great! And, thank you. Thank you for listening to my rant."

"Ranting is the perfect thing to do right now. Rant on, rant on! Considering the circumstances, ranting is the least you should do. Now, what is your idea?" she said with her captivating smile.

"What are the messages going around in your head about you, as a woman?" I asked her as I retrieved a pen buried at the bottom of my purse and moved the stained paper placemat closer, to begin recording some of the things coming out of my head.

She looked at me quizzically but still amused.

"Like what, exactly?"

"Just say the first things that come to your mind," I said.

After seeing the words I'd already written, she spoke quickly, in order to get it all out of her mind, as if someone might stop us. Eventually, we were almost saying them together as a chant. We had many of the same messages.

Women Are

Bad

Evil

Whores

Wrong

Valued Only For Their Body

Less Than A Commodity

Women Should Not Need Anything

Women Must Be Physically Perfect

Disdained For Intelligence

Disdained For Relationships And Intimacy

Disdained For Having Needs

Never Allowed To Feel Good About Themselves:

    If They Do, They Should Be Punished

Strictly Here To Provide Mothering Or Sex:

    If They Don't Provide Any Of These Things,

    They Should Be Hidden, Ignored, And Just Plain Not Exist

Never Allowed To Have Needs—Especially In Relationships

Responsible For Men's Unhappiness And Failures:

    But Not Their Successes

Bad If They Need A Primary Relationship

Given Anything They Want, If They Are Beautiful,

    But If They Are Not, They Should Not Be Seen

Either A Madonna Or A Whore

Inferior, Less Intelligent, Less Capable Than Men

Unable To Do Anything Right

Clueless And Need To Be Instructed

I LOOKED DOWN at what I'd written: That women are whores. That they're madonnas. It was right there—so close to the surface—within my psyche. But I knew that once you bring something to consciousness, you can see how wrong it is, and only then can you stop it. It was like my ex-husband's affairs: they were wrong, but there was no way to respond to that reality until it became conscious to me.

"It's like being part of the same shame club, but no one is in touch with it," Andrea said.

Then when she noticed me looking around, she said, "Is it an emperor's clothing thing? If we were to bring it to our own consciousness now, in this room, would everyone else in the room deny it or say it is just us?"

I nodded in sadness. "It's a sad state of affairs that you and I would even consider that they'd all deny it." I looked at the list. Suddenly I realized that this internal language came from inside us and was mirroring the patriarchal society outside us.

"Whoa, something just occurred to me, something that has been a mystery to me for some time," I said. "You know how others might say, if you judge something in others, it is because you have that in you?"

"Yeah! Isn't that annoying?" Andrea sounded sad and frustrated, and continued, "Because we don't treat women badly; in fact, we spend our careers helping them."

"Yes. What if our treatment of other women isn't to blame because we're looking for the demon in the wrong place? What if it doesn't have to do with our behavior toward other women?"

It was Andrea's turn to have goldfish eyes while waiting for me to finish my thought. She seemed to also get it as I continued.

"Yes!" she exclaimed.

I leaned forward and said quietly, but just as intensely, "It is what we say to *ourselves*."

We nodded vigorously. The excitement of this finding was in direct opposition to how sad it felt to me. It felt *so* sad. For the first time, I could see very clearly how I saw myself as a woman.

The placemat characterizations showed me how deep the rift went and that it was not just sexism: it was misogyny. The language went beyond discrimination and into abuse, ending in homicidal threats. I had been decimating my own sense of beauty and divinity. I wasn't treating other women badly, but I was destroying myself. And I was losing out on my life. I was losing out on things I loved.

Creating community, some idea of utopia with time to relax, pampering, wearing tons of color, crying, saying what I think and what I see, singing out loud, sleeping, seeing, reading, talking about love, swimming naked, being honest about magic, saying no to violent movies and yes to love.

It is a crime, I realized, that I "couldn't" enjoy being a woman. In my twenties, I couldn't enjoy running around in bikinis because I was too preoccupied reviewing whether I had cellulite. I see all these clients with their gorgeous silver hair, and they are so beautiful, yet they can't enjoy and accept themselves because they're comparing themselves to women in magazines.

"This pathetic placemat proves it. This is how we treat ourselves because we are women. The internal misogynist, this hater of women, directs this abuse inward," Andrea said and then deliberately bit down hard on a forkful of food.

"It's like what the Damanhurians say about the enemy," I said. "There is this voice whispering to us all of the time. And it's that of an internalized misogynist. And we are so brainwashed that, deep within ourselves, we've reinforced the belief that we are bad."

"How twisted is that?" Andrea said as she smiled and giggled in a low tone.

"Let's keep going?"

Yes, I thought. Let's keep going.

I stared at the placemat again. My sloppy handwriting, the folded edges, and the drops of maple syrup took over the whole thing. It looked war-torn. Suddenly, I felt myself shift into my role as a therapist. I thought of so many of the clients I saw on a daily basis who were dealing with this very thing externally. I thought of my domestic-violence clients, the women especially, who degraded themselves and continually begged deadly men for intimacy.

"Okay," Andrea said. "Just to play with this, let's say that someone walks into our office exhibiting these behaviors. If you witnessed this, what kind of a personality would you say engages in these kinds of beliefs and then acts based on them?"

"It would have to be a very disorganized personality structure," I said.

"Okay, go on."

"I see two personalities: one is a narcissistic personality disorder, and the other is a psychopathic or antisocial personality disorder—basically someone who seems to be totally full of himself or herself and also has no sense of morals."

"It's textbook," Andrea said.

She looked at the placemat. "And, not to forget, someone who splits. It's the classic Madonna-whore complex. There's no in-between here. Women are seen as one or the other; it's black or white. There is no gray area."

Splitting is a psychological symptom dreaded by therapists because, when it is operating, there is no way of knowing what will happen with a client. Clients who split can swing from adoration to demonization in an instant, and they are potentially dangerous because of the behavior that often accompanies their feelings of being let down.

I looked at her again. "Which developmental stage does splitting come from?"

"Something to do with not being able to go beyond the good mother/bad mother phase. You know, reconciling the two drives, love and hate. Who was it that said the more we are able to understand that everyone has good and bad parts, the more emotionally developed we are? Anyway, it must be object-relations theory; the child can't see the mother as human, right?"

"Yup." I said. "It's the relationship to abandonment that makes it complicated. If someone close to the child, like the mother, all of sudden has flaws, the child experiences an intense, irreconcilable sense of abandonment."

"Because the child has perceived or experienced the mother as being 'all good' up to this point, it is difficult for the child to understand and accept that the mother also has flaws. It's just like the perception of women and religion," Andrea said.

"Yes," I said, recalling my studies of divinity images and the lack of women icons in that context—unless they were virgins, of course.

"According to the Bible, having sex is considered a flaw or a weakness, and when women do have sex, their worthiness decreases dramatically. Having sex, and especially seeking or experiencing pleasure from sex, is known to set off this splitting behavior. It's a tricky situation because, while virgins make for great divinity images, traditionally they are also powerless creatures because they are denied access to themselves sexually—they're not allowed to fully be themselves without having shame," I said.

I mused to myself: the virgin's pseudo-power comes from a restraining of the self. If a woman eventually has sex, then at that point she loses her divinity. I looked down at that placemat again, and then Andrea spoke.

"And this shadow character we have inside us reflects a social norm," she said. "What this character's internal voice says is that the only way to relate to a woman is to dominate her, to have no tolerance for her humanity, and to demand that she have no initiative and no sense of individuality.

"You know, for a long time," I said, "I struggled with feeling that, in most of my interactions with others, men or women, my cooperation was more important to me than my individuality."

"Interesting. How did you eventually wake up to it?"

"I was on a stage, of all places, and Helen Palmer—an Enneagram expert—showed me that when I don't participate in making decisions, such as which restaurant I'd like to go to, it's a way of not taking responsibility for what I want. The responsibility for the decision would fall to the other person and often cause him or her to feel resentful. In the long run, with this behavior, I lose out on getting to know myself, while at the same time I keep others from getting to know the more honest, self-disclosing me. In a sense, I let this internal misogynist keep me from being myself. What would it look like to fully get that? Where would it take me?"

"That makes sense," Andrea said. "I wonder how much of our self we've lost by our own internal mirroring of the patriarchy?"

I began to think about my own internal misogynist. It didn't seem to have a care about the effects it was having on me. It had no moral code. And it had a kind of fantastical grandiosity. My internal misogynist was superior to me. I knew that whenever there's grandiosity in a relationship, it's usually a symptom of a narcissistic personality. It seems to say to one, I have to show that I am better than you because deep down I'm insecure.

"Maybe we keep attracting men who have these characteristics because they mimic our internal battle?" she continued, as if summing up the whole thing in one thought. "Why is it always such a shock to realize that these men can't be intimate?"

"Maybe this is what's happening to the world," I said. "Maybe, deep down, men ultimately feel insecure about themselves, and that's why they take this superior stance—a stance that's against mother earth, against women? Basically, if a man's peers consider him to be at all 'feminine,' that's a derogatory thing. Weak men are called pussies."

"Or, sometimes they're simply called a girl," Andrea said.

"I know it's not all men," I said, "but these things are symptoms that reflect the war inside us. And although it's not how we're treating other women, it is how we're treating ourselves."

It was sad, and it was also a relief. And now we knew what was wrong.

"I can't be intimate because I fear that, unless I'm obedient, I won't be loved," Andrea said. "Maybe that explains why I feel fat all of the time. I feel ashamed that I can't follow 'the rule' to be skinny."

"You feel fat, and I feel old."

"What an odd cycle we're in. How do we stop feeling this idea that 'I am less than'? What keeps us in this horrible cycle?"

"It's in our mind. But if it is all in our mind," I said, remembering the black box and the projector and the heartbeat, "we can wake up from this nightmare where misogyny is acceptable." I felt vitalized as I said these things.

"How to wake up is the challenge . . . ," she said.

"Yes. In waking up, we can look around us and see that there are men who do relate with love, and that we can create a kind of utopia, where men value women for their presence and their wisdom, and where we as women recognize and value our own internal power and strength. What if we lived in a world where women could choose to dress from the exuberance of feeling beautiful, a real expression of exaltation at being alive?"

"Amen," she said.

As Andrea spoke that one divine word, an incredible wave of gratitude moved through my body. So much energy was coming from my solar plexus area. It was enormous. I felt like I was reaping energy from an almost volcanic awakening inside the deepest level of myself. I was beginning to separate from the critic, and to regain what it was holding back. I could see and feel the power of the treasure that lay within.

When we realize that life is a mirror,
We stop reaching outward
to change the reflection
And turn to ourselves.
It is there that we can actually effect change.

INTERNALIZED MISOGYNY

Do the best you can, until you know better.
Then when you know better, do better.

MAYA ANGELOU, as relayed by Oprah Winfrey

After my energizing conversation with Andrea, I realized that because I didn't recognize the misogynist within me, it continued to reappear in myriad ugly forms. It mirrored my psyche back to me, and I saw that my psyche was filled with and dominated by the energy of the men that I'd attracted, a classic bardo. It was time for me to return to myself, to heal myself with the very tools I had long utilized for helping others to heal.

One of the first rules for initiating any healing process is to gain as much information as possible about the obstacle. One compelling view of this problem came from my friend Mike. He was a young, newly hired, full-time faculty member at a university where I was teaching on an adjunct, part-time basis. We had lengthy conversations in his campus office, situated in a building with long, narrow windows that offered a view of the well-manicured lawns.

"Mike," I said with excitement, "I had this amazing experience," and I told him about my conversation with Andrea.

"So now I'm trying to figure out all of this misogyny that I've discovered is actually inside me. I know that the next step is to get to the history of it all. I'm blown away by how unabashedly abused women are." I was a bit winded after I ran up the stairs the way I did when I was an undergrad, and also after blurting out the entire story of the placemat and the insights that Andrea and I had come to.

Mike looked at me with a broad smile. "Wow, Susie!" he said, "This is great. Are you familiar with Winnicott's work on subjective omnipotence?"

"Object relations at this level is not my area of expertise," I said and smiled. "Tell me more, if you would."

Pulling from his expertise all the theories that fit the symptoms, Mike had the capacity to quickly understand everything I was saying. He began to speak to me about object-relations theory according to British pediatrician and psychoanalyst Donald Winnicott.

"Winnicott theorized that the first developmental stage in childhood occurs when a child begins to signal for things he or she needs. If the child receives those things regularly, he or she begins to feel omnipotent. 'If I need something,' the child notices, 'I just get it!' Of course, this stage is preverbal, but you get my meaning. At some point, the child begins to wonder—not in thought, but by sensing—'Wait a minute. Am I alone? How do I figure that out?' The child begins to experience stress from this experience and reacts by biting the mother's breast or hitting the mother, who is providing the child with these desired things. This is where it gets really interesting.

"Depending on how the mother feels about herself, the child receives one of two messages. If the mother says, 'Stop,' and establishes a boundary for the child, the child, although reprimanded, receives relief because, by learning there is a boundary, the child gets an answer to the question, which is that, no, he or she is not *alone* in the universe; there are others. Mother is there, so everything is okay. But if, on the other hand, the mother doesn't stop the child, if she feels that for some reason she's responsible for the hitting or biting and is ashamed, then the child will keep pushing and poking in an attempt to find out if there are others out there. Ultimately, children under such circumstances might become dangerous in their search for a boundary, and, in extreme cases, they may exhibit antisocial or psychopathic tendencies. Essentially, it's the mother's degree of self-esteem that communicates to the child whether or not the child is alone in the universe."

"Wow!" I had a sense of where he was going.

"You could say that, deep down, the child wants the mother to say 'no' because unless the child hears the 'no,' he or she will continue to search and act out by hitting and biting, and so on. The child is looking for someone who will push back, someone who will finally give him or her the signal that the child so desperately needs—the signal that the child exists in a universe where there are others."

"And if that child's need remains unmet," I added, "the anxiety evoked from continuing to feel omnipotent and alone is so difficult that, to alleviate that anxiety, the child continues to test the environment by striking or lashing out."

"Exactly," Mike said.

"So the attitude of the mother or primary caregiver is everything here," I said.

"Yup."

What I began to realize is that this is the very dynamic that characterizes the relationship between our two genders in a world where men are in power to the exclusion of women. The male is often presented with, and even expected to have, this sense of total omnipotence.

The same dynamic occurs with the woman's internalized misogynist, which also views men *and* the self from that very perspective. This belief is one that says, I'm going to do whatever I want because I won't have to pay the consequences. That is, because the male sex is dominant, there is an unacknowledged sense of male omnipotence operating that seems to sanction men to behave in ways that are destructive to the planet, to women, to others, and so on.

This doesn't imply that all men are like this, but this behavior is often typical or even something society expects. So women have had to learn how to survive in a world where this pervasive view of male omnipotence remains largely unchallenged, and—even when acknowledged and challenged—is nonetheless quickly and repeatedly forgotten with the ongoing participation of men and women.

I knew this to be true because I recognized that, at the deepest level of myself, this film was playing on repeat, projected onto the ever-present walls of my life and who I think I am. It was the war between the masculine and feminine aspects in my own psyche that had produced and supported this horror movie. My masculine self was omnipotent within my own personality, while my feminine self was frightened into behaving, and this had all become entrained in my own non-helpful personality structure. Inside myself, I realized that my individuality as a female was getting lost in the interaction with the dominant, misogynistic part of me. And that shadow play characterizes what is happening on the planet.

"Among humanity, we're starting to see more and more evidence of these omnipotence and boundary issues play out, as I'm sure you already see. I was just thinking that because men are often given license to occupy these roles of omnipotence in society, we as women also internalize that. Creating—as I said before—our internal misogynist. As a systems therapist, this discovery of the internal misogynist seems significant."

"How so?" Mike said.

"If I can shift this part of me, then I believe it will shift all of the other parts of me," I said. "I'm reviving the collective intelligence of the feminine within myself."

The term "collective intelligence," which I had used with Mike, is one I had gotten from David Bohm, who, though now deceased, remains one of my favorite physicists. After participating in conferences and watching physicists debate each other and continue to cling to their own ideas—where they often wouldn't listen to other physicists or consider different viewpoints with much openness, but instead, would generally communicate with a style of defensiveness and criticism—Bohm grew very saddened at the thought of all of this intelligence being lost.

There was no way to collect or allow group wisdom to emerge and congeal, so Bohm formulated a way of interacting that he simply called dialogue. The word dialogue derives from the Greek *dialogos* (conversation), whose roots are *dia* (through) and *logos* (speech or reason). So a dialogue is a conversation with reason, or meaning, flowing through in a format that does not generally include debate.

According to Bohm's model, dialogue is a fluid process involving a group of participants engaging in free-flowing conversation, in an attempt to reach a common understanding through nonjudgmental witnessing of each speaker's viewpoint, a process that, in turn, can lead to new and deeper group understanding.

Instead of being a participant in the process of dialogue, I felt as if I had been in a lifelong debate with the masculine part of me and with men in general. Aspects of my feminine self in relationship with the masculine were being lost. But I started to see a healing intervention, and it involved this question: How might we make room for the voice of the feminine self?

I imagined a "guy movie" integrated with a fairytale. I saw the handsome prince with a gun in his hand and a look on his face that said, I'll love you if you are kind, obedient, and beautiful. Then I saw a tear fall down his face—a tear of loneliness and also a tear evoked by his frustration of being unable to relinquish the gun, which represented his threat to others and the power that comes from believing oneself to be omnipotent. I saw the princess covered in cinders in a corner, waiting and hoping she would be seen as a princess—an heiress of equal power, and not as the enemy or the one in need of protection. I saw both of these characters in pain, each hoping one wouldn't kill or abandon the other, each holding a deep longing for the other.

When you find where the disunion lies within you,
it starts the path to a real relationship with the self.
Dig for your truth, so you can be ecstatically horrified.

HER STORY

The hatred of women affects us in ways that no other hatred does because it strikes at our innermost selves. It is located where the private and public worlds intersect.

JACK HOLLAND

I pulled out the placemat again and put it on my coffee table. The white crumpled paper looked thin on the painted red surface of this beloved piece of Chinese furniture that had belonged to my grandmother. Provided I could read the clues, our simple scribbles on this fragile page had become a treasure map that shed light on the rocky terrain of my psyche, a land that, until now, had been impossible to negotiate in the dark. The mirroring it evoked was horrifying yet inspiring because not only could I see the prejudice in my mind, but I was also reminded of the therapeutic tools I had readily available for negotiating this interior pilgrimage. What had felt like glue—once in the form of an imprisoning box and now revealed as a journey—was becoming less and less intimidating.

Our placemat expressed chilling statements such as, "Women are strictly here to provide mothering or sex; if they don't provide any of these things, they should be hidden, ignored, and just plain not exist." Clearly there was a homicidal threat lurking in the murky depths, and I needed to find the roots of that fear and dig them out. I was too awake now to allow an unconscious terror to haunt me any longer and keep me from my dreams.

I knew this mortal threat—this idea that I have to die or be killed if I'm not loved or useful to a man—didn't consciously arise from anything I'd experienced as a child or anything that had been said to me. Nonetheless, I knew the seed for the idea was there. During my divorce, I had spent many a morning with an irrational terror that I was going to be killed.

Watching one of my female relatives appear terrified when she thought she'd made what was a minor mistake in phrasing while speaking to her husband gave me the feeling that I was not alone. With just a fleeting look, she silently communicated that everything she set out to do had to be done very carefully or the consequences would be dire.

I could feel my mother's deep fears as well, and I knew that her husband and her father both deeply intimidated her. Sometimes when she gestured I could see her shake with a fear that suggested she was afraid she'd said or done the wrong thing. Because there was no physical violence in our home or in the home of my terrified female relative, there was no crime to be named—yet the behaviors of these women suggested that they feared something that seemed to threaten their survival.

So it could only be a residue from the past. It was psychological phenomena that had traveled through generations, which, in the language of Bowen's family systems theory, is called a multigenerational (or family) transmission process. But the question is, how deep did this rabbit hole go? How far back in history did this terrifying thought have to travel to arise from my psyche now, at the dawn of the twenty-first century?

MY FATHER'S FATHER, Bill, was charismatic and loved by the community for his charm, but he was a different man when he came home. He ruled his wife and children with intimidation. While men in the family had to be physically under his dominion, where they were beaten, their fate differed from the emotionally disturbing treatment that awaited the women.

"The women were considered morons," my father said when I interviewed him for this book. "He wouldn't let mother buy groceries because he was convinced she'd be irresponsible with their money. She had to make meals with whatever he brought home."

According to my father, the most intimidating form of punishment my grandfather meted out at home was the silent treatment. "You were treated as if you weren't present," he told me.

He said that one day, without provocation, his father imposed this exact punishment on the only other woman in the family besides his wife: his daughter, who was his eldest child. Now, my aunt is also one of the most intuitive women I know, with a great deal of sensitivity and intelligence. One particular day—and no one seems to know why—my grandfather just stopped speaking to her at all. According to my father, sadly, like a lamb headed to slaughter, she continued to come to dinner, where he'd never address or say anything to her directly but would speak about her as if she weren't there. From then on, this behavior of my grandfather's continued for years. When he said anything involving her, it was usually in the form of comments about her ineptitude and how inferior she was. So she often left family meals in tears but eventually had to completely stop eating dinner with them and, instead, began to eat alone in her own room, each evening.

The theory the family had about this, decades later, was that because this first occurred when she reached puberty, perhaps my grandfather could not handle her emerging sexuality as a young woman, and therefore he chose to simply shut her out. But I imagined far worse.

She married when she was quite young and became pregnant in the context that was commonly referred to then as "out of wedlock."

Her brother (my father Jim) walked her down the aisle because her father was said to have been "out hunting" that day, and her mother also refused to come. Her mother had told her before the wedding to never come back home because she had disgraced the family.

One day, after my father had seen her with her newborn baby, he was able to get the family to come forward and reconnect with her.

"She finally reconciled with our father, but I couldn't ever forgive him," my father said with resignation. "Because I hadn't ever forgiven him, I cried throughout his funeral when he died. I was so angry at how he had treated her."

Before his death, my grandfather was able to reconcile with my aunt. It's a moving story, and she sheds a tear when she mentions it. However, his heavy presence within the family dynamic remains in the consciousness of all his offspring.

It could be reasonably argued that my parents unconsciously chose each other out of a sense of cultural familiarity and also because of the sexism, misogyny, and deep sense of social shame that existed within my mother's family line as well.

My mother witnessed her father consistently put down her mother, who was quite intelligent. She remembers my grandmother sitting alone late at night, drunk, and arguing with an imaginary husband after her actual husband (my grandfather) had gone to bed. As a result, both my mother's sister and my mother worked to make sure they weren't his targets, and they devised ways to avoid his disdain.

My mother's way of coping was to attempt to live up to his intensely high expectations. She became a star tennis player and went to Stanford, where she played college tennis. She seemed to carry an unconscious belief that her father loved her mainly for her accomplishments. While she was constantly terrified of letting him down, she also watched him publicly disdain her mother.

Among the many terrors my mother held around how she could disappoint her father, the worst concerned her fear of becoming pregnant out of wedlock. According to my mother, if a woman had sex without being married and others found out, that woman would be ostracized—even from her own family. Furthermore, the entire family would be disgraced. Her father made it very clear that she would be disgraced if this ever happened to her. He also made it clear that if this ever happened, he would split off from her, the daughter whom he seemingly loved above everyone else.

My mother often talked with me about this terror. When I was a child of less than five years, I remember, I would punch my stomach in attempts to make sure there were no child inside of me. Somehow even then, at such an early age, I had already ingested the message.

My parents were products of their upbringing, and, in keeping with that, my father often treated my mother as if she were a moron. He says that when I was about five, since he had no model from which to raise a daughter, he ceased interacting with me as much as possible. He said he left it up to my mother to parent me. I recall approaching him only to have to leave in shock because he would wave me away and refer me back to my mother, while, at the same time, he'd lavish his attention on my brothers.

The transmission process was clearly evident in my family and was probably minor compared to that of other families. But the fear was deeper than that.

AS A VERY faint bell rang in my mind, I recalled a memory concerning one of my ancestors. This ancestor was some sort of counsel or attorney involved with the Salem witch trials. My mother and my paternal grandmother had traced both sides of my family back several hundred years. I remembered my mom pulling out old family photo albums in my father's workroom while talking over the phone with unsuspecting, distant cousins whom she'd discovered through her research.

"Do you still have all that family genealogy stuff that you put together ages ago?" I said on the phone to my mother.

"I do," she said. "I can give you what I have. What do you need it for?"

"I'm trying to find that ancestor who was an attorney in the Salem witch trials."

"Oh yes," she said with a curious tone. "He was a Herrick, and, interestingly enough, he was related to your grandmother, even though your grandfather Bill had Herrick as his surname and her maiden name was Harvey."

"Interesting that dad's mom was related to some Herricks as well, and they were involved in the Salem witch trials," I said.

"Yes, she married into a family that she was distantly related to, so that made her husband some kind of distant cousin," my mother said.

"Wow. I'll come over and get the stuff from you."

I found going through all the information she'd collected to be both enchanting and educational. Names and dates on the branch line of family trees and the relationships of my ancestors came alive via newspaper announcements, articles, and letters. Like the methods of any good time-traveler, time was, in this case, being spun backward, in a sense, through my family's American and English history, and some of those moments resurfaced quite naturally.

I had a great-great-uncle who stole horses and a great-great-aunt—they weren't related to one another—who was a famous opera star. Though some of these relations were quite distant generations, I found it fascinating that there was a U.S. President in there somewhere, and, even farther back, there were kings of Scotland and Wales. I could imagine the corsets, the wooden houses, the landscapes, the parties, the tragedies, the successes, and the courage so many of them must have had. I was a product of brave pioneers dating back to 1066 and earlier. One of my ancestors fought with Harold II, the last Anglo-Saxon King of England, against William the Conqueror, who led the Norman Conquest.

Since I was the only redhead in our family for generations, one of my mother's favorite stories she'd tell me when I was a child was that a Native American tribe had captured my great-great-aunt (my great-grandmother's older half-sister), at the age of two, because of her red hair. As the story goes, they did this because they thought she was a goddess. I want to make sure to point out here that this story was from the perspective of my family, which wasn't necessarily the perspective of the Native American tribe. When rereading it recently, I thought of the ironic parallel between my ancestral history and how I was in some way attempting to restore to our family lore the belief that there is divinity in the female—or, that it at least be recognized. Furthermore, my great-grandmother's father was the one who had "rescued" her, a metaphor for what was to happen to me later.

Then I found a note about the attorney in the Salem witch trials. It's hard to describe the feeling I had when I looked at all the information that was available, together with my mother's research and, later, the online material. The witch trials were a major historical event, and I had even visited Salem myself. But now, learning of this genealogical connection brought the horror of this event much closer. In fact, at least five Herricks were involved in those witch trials.

George and Joseph Herrick had the most significant roles, and they played a central part in the proceedings. Joseph was the law enforcement officer, or constable, who made arrests, and George was marshal of the court and acted as one of the main prosecutors in the trials.

The accusers had persuaded Joseph of the rightness of their cause, and so it was he who made the arrests. But at some point he became skeptical. In one of the cases, he became an advocate for one of the accused, which was probably quite dangerous for him personally. In the end, he became a leader in the opposition movement. A court record in relation to Joseph mentions his parents, who had been fined "for aiding and comforting an excommunicated person, contrary to order." Furthermore, there was another Herrick who was on the jury and also a Herrick in-law who was one of the accused.

Those witch trials were a mystery and a terrifying example of the way society viewed women in early American history, particularly because women accused of witchcraft were executed then at a rate five times that of men. The three original women accused in these infamous trials near Salem were quite vulnerable to ridicule and discrimination. One was a homeless woman and beggar, one was ill and could not attend church and was in a legal controversy or family feud with the accuser's family, and one was a woman of color. Women who stood out as odd or different were those most at risk of being accused. In other words, if women weren't clearly following the traditions of the society of their time, they would easily find themselves subject to hanging or the proverbial burning at the stake. As it turned out, all of the innocent who had been accused during those trials were hanged. This theme of different, unusual, or nonconforming women being brutalized was common throughout Western civilization.

Similar horrors had been going on for centuries in Europe. After examining history during the classical period of witch-hunts in Early Modern Europe and Colonial North America, it became evident to me how some of my ancestors could have easily been caught up in them. Those witch-hunts began in the fourteenth century and continued until the eighteenth century, and about forty to sixty thousand were executed. It is estimated that 75 to 80 percent of those killed were women. It was a frightening time for women who lived on the fringes, particularly those who considered themselves healers.

Women were being tried and brutally executed not only for utilizing natural medicines, but, at times, merely for being women who were sexually attractive. In a sense, during that period, if you happened to arouse a man on the wrong day—a man who was from the wrong crowd or was a psychopath, for that matter—according to the prevailing society, he could safely call you a "witch." You would then be considered guilty until proven innocent because the thinking at the time was that the basis of all this was "women's proneness to lust and therefore to demonic temptation."

The fact that there was public hysteria and support for this prejudice and discrimination in a Puritan stronghold is not surprising. To have relatives that participated to the extent that mine allegedly did was personally chilling, and it was easy to see how that could have a generational impact.

I found it unnerving to consider that if I had lived then, I would have certainly been a target. I'm a green-eyed redhead, and if one adds in all of my "odd," or uncommon, life perspectives and skills, I would have been taken to the gallows in no time. From this angle of our family transmission process, my own thoughts, which I'd recently noted on that placemat, didn't seem so far-fetched.

HAVING STUDIED ENGLISH history as a child, I was intrigued to take a look at my ancestors there. The Herrick family tree in America began with a Henry Herrick, who was the fifth son of William Herrick, an English nobleman. Either he, or a cousin of his by the same name, immigrated to the New World (it seems that both cousins did, with the other immigrating to Virginia). After he arrived in America from England, Henry settled in Salem, Massachusetts, in 1629.

It was through Henry's father, William, that my mother was able to trace some of the family origins dating to before 1066. William was a jeweler for Elizabeth I, Queen of England. He had a peerage and land holdings, which now constitute what is reportedly a lovely museum—one that I've not yet visited.

The fact that William worked for the queen is of interest to me because I am one of her fans. She was one of the most powerful figures in English history, if not world history—a woman, and a redhead to boot.

I imagine serving as her jeweler to have been quite the job, especially considering her vast wealth and love of adornment. Her personality, her intelligence, and her whims would very likely have had significant impact on William's life.

Now just how much impact Elizabeth I had on my ancestral transmission process I will never know, but her impact on history, as a woman trying to adeptly respond to patriarchy, was groundbreaking and sad. She was clever, to say the least.

She had what I would call a "misogynistic quandary" when she took the throne. If she were to marry, a man would rule her; yet, as a single woman, people might question her strength to rule, and thus her ministers tried to marry her off. She considered this quandary from the viewpoint that she needed to do whatever it took to keep her power. She noticed that society had practice at worshipping a virgin, the Virgin Mary. She realized that men could tolerate being ruled by a woman who was nonsexual. Therefore she capitalized on her reputation as a purported virgin and termed herself "the virgin queen." This became popularized such that even the colony Virginia was named in her honor.

What this "communicates" to me—not to mention what it might "communicate" to society in general now—is that the minute a woman had sex she relinquished her power.

Ironically, William's nephew was Robert Herrick, a poet who wrote the poem titled "To the Virgins, To Make Much of Time," a work that has been praised over the centuries for its artistic description of the Latin phrase *carpe diem*, or "seize the day."

> Then be not coy, but use your time,
> And, while ye may, go marry;
> For, having lost but once your prime,
> You may forever tarry.

The poem warns young women to seize love now because they will no longer be lovable when they are old and ugly. A male poet could use this as a metaphor and perhaps as social commentary, but for women at that time in history, this societal attitude and stigma was a serious reality for women. Whoever a woman married determined her safety and treatment in society—it could even mean the difference between life and death. How a woman had or did not have sex determined her life circumstances and even her very survival.

I had to ask the obvious questions: Why? Why was sex such a bad thing and a forbidden subject? Why were life-and-death issues tied to it? And why was a woman's whole life socially determined by how she dealt with it? Why was sex culturally disempowering for women, and particularly if her sexual behavior occurred out of wedlock? It was a mystery to me how by maintaining virginity one could be worshipped, but by having sex one could be disgraced. Since the act of sexual intercourse is critical to the propagation and continuation of human life, why should I, or any woman, be ashamed of our very nature as a sexual being?

SO I DUG further, and this time I found some research that answered my questions. I knew the Old Testament blamed women for "the original sin," by depicting Eve as the evil temptress who seduced Adam into taking a bite of the forbidden apple, which resulted in their banishment from the Garden of Eden. For millennia, human culture has perpetrated a perception of women as having a deficit of character in contrast to men. The effect of this cultural edict is broadly common in practice if not knowledge, and it relates to all of the ways in which women are discriminated against.

When the tribes of Israelites rose to power, the role of women in that historical region of the Middle East changed. Women went from being property owners and sovereign citizens to becoming the property of men. Furthermore, not only did women's sexuality fall from the perception of it as something divine, it fell to the complete jurisdiction of men. The only respectable roles for women then were as a virgin daughter or a wife because a woman's sexuality had become the property of her father or her husband. In other words, a woman and her sexuality went from being worshiped to being owned by men and treated as chattel, thereby severing the ties between divinity and female sexuality. If a woman had sex with someone other than those who owned her, she was condemned to death. This answered the question of why it was important to be a virgin or a wife—and dangerous to be otherwise. However, it still didn't answer why being sexual and having sex was shameful. I kept searching.

When we examine the time during which Christianity came into power, it becomes evident that the gap between sexuality and respectability, let alone divinity, had grown even greater. Celibacy eventually came to be considered superior to marriage and a way to emulate the nonsexual image and reputation attributed to Christ and to his virgin mother, Mary. Abstaining from sex was virtuous for anyone not procreating, and the attraction to flesh was a sin. Marriage was a protection from sin because those who could not otherwise control their sexual behavior could have sanctioned sex within the confines of the marital bed. However, Christian marriage was a marriage with abstinence thrown in as well because, even though the church sanctioned sexual relations with one marriage partner only, the sexual act itself was sanctioned for the sole purpose of procreation within the marriage context. Therefore, in accord with church doctrine, if marriage partners chose not to procreate, they were not supposed to have sexual relations.

Furthermore, the responsibility for respectable interaction lay almost solely on the shoulders of women. According to Saint Augustine, men's erections were considered involuntary, and therefore women were expected to be the ones to halt sinful sexual relations. Their expressions of sexual desire were scrutinized and criticized more than those of men because women's desires were purported to be within their conscious control. Ironically, this stemmed from the belief that Adam merely took a bite out of the apple to be nice to Eve so that she did not have to face the sin alone, and that Eve had committed this sinful act out of a lack of personal control and will.

Then women were not only the property of men, but they were also required to uphold religious and spiritual standards and were severely judged if they didn't. This created an even more substantial double standard between the sexes because women were held responsible for the sins of sex, whereas men were not.

Having sexual relations before marriage would destroy a woman's reputation because it meant that she'd fallen from being regarded as a possible madonna, like Mary, to being labeled a whore. Furthermore, if a woman even hinted that she wanted or enjoyed sex in any way, her reputation as a pious Christian would be forever lost.

As I combed through the research, I felt at risk even reading the information. *How was this possible?* I thought, in disbelief. How could we allow the vestiges of this to remain alive in our psyche today? With such fear, with such terror, I could now see why, in her book *Women Who Run With The Wolves*, author Clarissa Pinkola Estes wrote, "Wildlife and the Wild Woman are both endangered species." Raw feminine intelligence and worthiness—anything innate, animalistic, anything related to women as autonomous sexual beings, as mothers, and so on—has been under male purview, in a male-dominated world that has pronounced itself superior and has thereby assumed the role of standard-bearer, over thousands of years.

IT NOW MAKES sense to me why men I was interested in confused me and why they seemed confused too. Attraction is instinctual, but when mixed with the cultural feelings of shame, it is almost impossible to reconcile. I realized the split was operating in full force for me during my earliest years of dating because, as I became a sexually attractive young woman, I found men who clearly seemed to adore me, yet when I responded to their attention, they would respond in turn with disdain. In the environment of the religious organization in which I was raised, I was considered "sexy," and I heard second-hand from some of my male peers that they'd overheard gossip that this perception was "a problem" with me. Something was wrong with me because I was sexual. I became a symbol for something within these men that they themselves could not deal with.

I was devastated when I learned of this during those early years, and I then concluded I needed to change because it meant my sexiness and sexual attraction to men were things to be ashamed of. This was a dilemma because my sexuality afforded me the attention and personal power that my hormones were so desperately screaming for, yet that attention was coupled with shame and degradation. Eventually I was able to downplay it, as I worked very hard to not be seen in that way. I see now, at the height of my youth and attractiveness and my sexuality, that I felt ashamed of it. This made me see that if I—as a woman who grew up in Northern California, one of the most politically free and liberated places on the planet—continued to feel this way, then not only was that a personal loss for me, but how much worse it must be elsewhere for all women and men, in general.

I saw that ultimately it was my own mind that kept me from enjoying the freedoms that I actually had. Furthermore, it kept me from enjoying the natural beauty that I had. As I look back on pictures of myself at those times, the idea that I felt so imperfect, limited, and powerless now seems utterly ridiculous.

I can see now how the first prostrations I performed at the lake and the requests I had made to the planet Venus years ago, at Lake Namtso, symbolized a catalyzing move for me on a level or dimension that, quite likely, I still don't fully understand. Venus, as an embodiment of the goddess, represented the possibility of healing this rift between me and my feminine. Known as Aphrodite in Greek mythology, the name Venus is Roman and means "goddess of love." She is beautiful, ageless, and alluring. She may have arisen even earlier in herstory than the dates conjured according to the mythology of ancient Greece. She has connections to the deities Hathor, Astarte, Ishtar, and Inanna, and it has been suggested that the goddess Venus was far more powerful at one time than how she is depicted within the Greek pantheon.

She is divine *and* sexual. This makes her a specifically healing archetype for women who have been taught, in accord with the views of their respective cultures and religions, that these two aspects are mutually exclusive. On the other hand, Aphrodite, seemingly free in totality, has nothing to be ashamed of. Furthermore, that which makes Aphrodite divine is exactly what I had thought questionable and shameful: her exquisitely tempting female sexual power.

At Lake Namtso, I hadn't been fully aware of the history and lineage, not to mention the ramifications and the power, of asking Aphrodite herself—Venus—to wake me up. It is interesting, though, that Inanna, her predecessor, was called queen of the sky, that Namtso is called sky lake or lake of heaven, and that the dakinis are called sky-goers or sky-dancers as well. Perhaps all of these sky-going messengers were from Aphrodite, who, along with the owl, my ducks, and that damned eagle too, were *all* prodding me to wake up.

I was looking for freedom and power. I was just beginning to understand that feminine power is always present, and that there was something in me that was sapping that power. If anything, the symbolism represented by Venus, Aphrodite, Inanna, and Chomolungma was pointing me in one direction: to heal the rift in my mind, to recognize and reconfirm the inherent divinity, or true unity, of the male and female aspects of my psyche.

The apparent rift is not only the product of illusion within me, it is also a rift displayed between the genders and, in a much broader way, a rift at a global level. Across cultures, we've treated "mother earth" in the same way women have been treated. Thousands of years of feminine intelligence and wisdom have been lost. This rift is dangerous and it has obvious global ramifications. My hope is that the possibility of restoring or resurrecting this is not too late.

I was reminded of what my friend Kate Wolf-Pizor once said. "One way to recover from the patriarchy is to discover the uniqueness of being a woman and then to accept it as real. It doesn't matter if only you see it. The point . . . is to put what we have to offer as women back into motion."

In other words, what we women need now, in order for healing to begin, is to restore the uniqueness of the feminine and set it into motion within the public arena and the environment as a whole.

There are no enemies here; there is only loss and ignorance, and it is now time to fully acknowledge the wound and begin to mend it.

As long as we are on earth, the love that unites us
will bring us suffering by our very contact with one
another, because this love is the resetting of a Body of
broken bones; even saints cannot live with saints on
this earth without some anguish, without some pain
at the differences that come between them.
There are two things men [and women] can do about
the pain of disunion with other men [and women],
they can love or they can hate. Hatred recoils from the
sacrifice and sorrow that are the price of resetting the
bones—it refuses the pain of reunion.

THOMAS MERTON

THE MIRROR

One does not become enlightened by imagining figures
of light, but by making the darkness conscious.

C.G. JUNG

After all of this research and conversation, I felt I had a good handle on how pervasive, mesmerizing, and insidious misogyny can be. I could see the damage it manifested over generations and how that had precluded me from a developing healthy view of relationship within myself, let alone with anyone else. I had to engage the enemy, my internal misogynist, and I had to put together a plan to do it.

One day, after becoming curious and then searching for the term "internalized misogyny," I found this definition by Daleo and Riggs:

> Internalized misogyny explains some of women's psychology in terms of the values, behaviors, and beliefs women experience due to the identification and internalization of the misogynist culture at large. Internalized misogyny can be used as a basis of understanding for a variety of women's experiences.

I wrote the following in my journal, summarizing my insights about this misogynistic part inside me:

In sum, I have an uninformed critic inside me that's afraid of omnipotence. It speaks to the feminine part of me, convincing me that I am fundamentally flawed and should be ashamed of my femininity. Due to millennia filled with patriarchal cultural transmissions that I inherited, as well as my own life experiences, my feminine side truly, if unconsciously, believes this message to be true. My insides are expressing the patriarchy. There is a hierarchical structure within me: my masculine was dominant and ruled over my feminine by using tactics like threats and humiliation.

How do I survive? By being as invisible as possible while simultaneously hoping to have my needs met. I have an ego or personality structure designed to keep me in a constant state of regard for others, at my expense, meaning I allow very little or no room for my individuality, let alone for my feminine side. I am suffering with low self-esteem, learned helplessness, and intergenerational post-traumatic stress disorder (PTSD— that is, my irrational fear of homicide and abuse), and I have some characteristics of dependent personality disorder. I feel at-risk every time I make a decision, act in my self-interest, or express my creative self.

In Damanhurian terms, I've believed in the enemy and, as a result, have kept myself from myself and lost out on my own sense of originality, my sense of connection to the vital force of creativity, and to the basis of life. My internal dragon has been hanging onto my luminous pearl—my beautiful divine self—desperately trying to keep me safe and to protect my vulnerability. Now I had to convince myself to let go, so the entirety of my internal self could reap the healing benefits of the light I emanated, like the unwavering light of the planet Venus in the sky at twilight.

UPON DISCOVERING WHAT was amiss, it was easy for me to come up with what I wanted for myself. I wrote my own treatment plan and goals:

- *Improve internal relationship between masculine and feminine parts*
- *Raise self-esteem*
- *Reduce PTSD symptoms*
- *Develop tools to directly meet my needs*
- *Foster an environment where I can learn about and improve my uncommon abilities, such as my visions*
- *Someday initiate a forum of the world's religious leaders and wealthiest people to learn what women from all ranks and walks of life think we can and need to do to heal the planet.*

When I wrote this last item, I felt stupid, but I promised myself that I would just write it down anyway. So there it was in writing, reflecting to me what my heart really wanted.

When one gets a truthful reflection of one's self,
One is goaded into action.

INTERVENTION

An integrated individual is one who carries their own dark shadow of undesirable qualities, frees those around them from their projections, and by so doing actually transforms a fraction of the evil in the world. When they carry their own bright shadow, they take up their courage, their strength, and their dignity, and their own imaginative insight, and refuse to be bowed down by burdens that others are unknowingly projecting on to them.

IRENE CLAREMONT DE CASTILLEJO

I n a therapeutic context, the word *intervention*, as I define it here, means an action that produces a potentially significant impact on a system in order for it to change for the better.

Like Anansel had done, it was time that I faced the enemy head-on. The intervention I prescribed for myself was to speak to my own internal misogynist, my most dangerous internal dragon, with truth. However, in the process, I learned that how I expressed the truth would prove challenging.

TWO MEN I had studied extensively had spoken the truth so effectively that it made my heart sing: Mahatma Gandhi and Martin Luther King, Jr. I was familiar with them not only because of my work as a peace activist but also in relation to my work as a marriage and family therapist, mediator, teacher, and trainer of therapists and mediators. In my mind, these men were communication geniuses, although, ironically, it was these two men, not women, to whom I looked for wisdom. Perhaps I sought their wisdom because they were members of the sex I was trying to understand. Or, maybe my search was an attempt to navigate the masculine part of myself. Either way, these wise men knew how to address the perilous game of survival at this deep male level, and they knew how to prevail without advocating violence.

After an exotic tea lunch at a friend's, I waited for my ride and browsed her giveaway bookshelf in the hallway. I pulled out a Thomas Merton book of Gandhi's writings, opened it to a random page, and found this:

> The first principle of non-violent action is that of
> non-cooperation with everything humiliating.

Although I may have seen the sentence before, it now struck me as the answer I was looking for. The part in the movie *Gandhi*, where Gandhi, who was played by Ben Kingsley, tells the British, "You must, in the nature of things, humiliate us to control us," now also made complete sense to me.

As we drove away, the memory of Kingsley's voice reverberated in my mind, that "You must . . . humiliate us to control us."

When I got home, I looked up the verb "humiliate." I found that it denotes a form of diminishing someone, perceiving or treating someone as if they are less than or beneath oneself or others. Or, according to Merriam-Webster's online dictionary, the meaning is "to reduce to a lower position in one's own eyes or others' eyes." It stems from the word "humus," which means earth. I remembered my history lessons about feudalism and realized that our ancestors fought for distinction by making their way to the top, by dominating others, by making others lower. Those that worked the earth were the ones they regarded as lowest.

For centuries, the East Indian culture had a very hierarchical caste system. The British came in and, quite easily, exerted psychological control over the Indian population by making them feel inferior to the British. I could see what Gandhi was faced with: institutionalized

British superiority that dictated Indian inferiority, which is astonishing when you consider that, at the time, there were some one thousand two hundred British civil servants who were dominating approximately 350 million Indians.

How could one control others by subjecting them to humiliation? I pondered. Then I looked up the word again, but this time in a thesaurus. "Ah ha!" I declared aloud, and my cat jumped. The noun "humiliation" is a synonym for shame. I knew from my therapeutic work that shame is one of the most vulnerable of feelings because it has such significant social consequences.

"Have you no shame?" I remembered a friend's mother saying once.

Shame, of course, is that feeling inside us that we do not want to feel because it alerts us to the idea that there is something about us that is socially unfit or possibly something intrinsically wrong with us. It's not the feeling that we've done something wrong; that's guilt—but the feeling that something might actually be unchangeably wrong with us. For example, if your parents shame you for a potty-training accident you have at a young age, or if your peers during your teenage years shame you for your personal appearance, and the emotions you experience as a result are left unintegrated, they can cause you to feel as if there is something inherently wrong with you, as opposed to understanding those as feelings that can change, or that you are loveable regardless.

Gandhi believed that all people are intrinsically good, and that no human is inherently bad or evil. Because humiliation attacks and undermines the healthy, or true, sense of self, Gandhi refused to cooperate with it. He accomplished this by simply separating an individual from his or her actions. To Gandhi, the British themselves weren't evil. Rather, the evil was in the laws they'd instituted and the evil manner in which people carried them out.

What this meant to me was that when one stops allowing oneself to be humiliated or feel humilation, one is saying to others: I refuse to label or call *you* intrinsically bad, or to accept it if you label or call me the same. I'm not judging you, but I am judging *your actions*. It is your ignorant actions that I will not condone or adjust to.

Now I understood why Gandhi could treat everyone with such kindness. He refused to shame anyone or react to anyone's shaming actions toward himself. He wrote, "Man's nature is not essentially evil. Brute nature has been known to yield to the influence of love. You must never despair of human nature."

One day I was given the opportunity to put these lessons I was learning into practice in real life. It was when I was a single woman and was participating in a multi-day workshop. I'd become a little bored, so I began looking around, "Who do I think is cute here?" There was a really tall guy who sort of reminded me of Leonard Nimoy's character, Spock, in *Star Trek*. I felt drawn to him and made it my goal to try to get into a group or one-on-one session with him, but it just never came to pass. Around that time, I was reading a book by the relationship aficionado Dr. Harville Hendrix. In his book *Keeping the Love You Find*, Hendrix gives the reader some assignments and recommends that one practice them in real life. I kept speculating: why is it that I can attract all these men, but I can never seem to attract the guy I actually want?

Inspired by the book, I decided to share these thoughts with this total stranger, the handsome man I'd spied earlier and had then finally approached during a break in the workshop. I vented to him in this vein when he blurted out in choppy, but emphatic words, "That's because you shoot darts at men when you meet them!"

It was a surreal thing for someone to say, but I thought about it for the remainder of the workshop, and I pieced together that, in fact, I had been doing that very thing because I felt shame around attraction. Unconsciously, though not unreasonably, I had concluded from the family ancestral transmission process that I should not show that I felt chemistry with men. A fear of expressing my feelings had been transmitted to me as an unconscious warning system: I couldn't let men think I was interested, or else, I'd been led to believe, they would feel that they were better than me and then not like me. My feelings of attraction, I believed, made me bad and therefore unattractive because "women can't be good and sexual at the same time." As I looked deeper, I could see that what was really happening was that I was exuding attraction for men along with feeling shame—or I was projecting "darts" at them at the same time—so I was sending them a very confusing message. While this was a horribly sad realization, it was nonetheless great news to have the insight. At that point I could begin to make the unconscious conscious and transform those ancient messages.

So I stopped cooperating with the part of me that demanded I be ashamed of these attractions, the self-bullying part of me. I affirmed to myself, "It *is* really healthy to be attracted, and it *is* really healthy to be in relationship."

Martin Luther King, Jr. was an admirer of Gandhi and fashioned a great deal of his work on the principles that Gandhi embodied. King wrote,

> Gandhi was probably the first person in history to lift the love ethic of Jesus above mere interaction between individuals to a powerful and effective social force on a large scale. Love for Gandhi was a potent instrument for social and collective transformation. It was in this Gandhian emphasis on love and nonviolence that I discovered the method for social reform that I had been seeking.

Studying both of these men and their work gave me more insight into their interventions and methods. These great humans excelled specifically by refusing to adjust to behavior that was wrong, while at the same time not holding hatred toward those who behaved in such ways. Thus King's discerning observation, "Human salvation lies in the hands of the creatively maladjusted," provided me with startling clarity and offered me an intervention.

I would no longer adjust to the patriarchal paradigm of misogynistic underpinnings that caused such injustice and suffering in my internal world and my culture, nor would I continue to feign respect for the actions of those with whom I didn't agree, although I would respect them as human beings. It was necessary that I not allow my feelings of maladjustment to result in the usual fight response of the lizard-like brain, but, instead, that I come to the loving alternative generated through the creativity of my mind.

Another insight of King's afforded me the steadfast courage to move forward. I had taken the train to San Francisco, to meet a friend at a teahouse there, as I so often did. I arrived early and noticed a park below the teahouse, so I followed the compelling sound of nearby water to lead me there. How enchanting the soothing sound was—rushing, falling water, filling that area of the city with its natural melody. The site itself is a magnificent memorial to Martin Luther King, Jr., with the largest fountain on the West Coast, at Yerba Buena Gardens, right in downtown San Francisco.

I made a mental note to thank those artists and others who insist on making sure that these sorts of creative expressions of universal truth and beauty transpire in the midst of extremely expensive and often grim urban real estate.

As I entered this chanced-upon sanctuary, the surrounding air felt cool and moist, and the sound of water offered respite from the world outside. While walking along this enclave constructed beneath a huge reflecting pool, I saw the twelve glass panels where excerpts from King's speeches are engraved in multiple languages. My cool skin tingled as I took in the resounding beauty and significance of the wise words that had been so carefully etched into those walls. The dancing sparkles of waterdrops from the fountain kissed my arms as I walked. I saw that truth was everywhere.

I noticed King had died twenty-six days before my sixth birthday, and then I remembered the day of his funeral, when I'd walked with my father and so many others in a memorial march. My dad was all dressed up then in a suit with a white shirt, and his warm, loving hand felt so large compared to mine. He made me feel safe on such a mournful day. Even as a young child I could feel the beauty as well as the terrible sadness—a day of deep pain and sorrow and, at the same time, awe that such a human had even existed. My father spoke at the gathering, and I'm sure my mother was beaming as she watched her handsome husband give tribute to one of the greatest humans ever. I think my father felt alive and proud just to be present on earth in order to offer homage to this noble man.

NOW, SO MANY years later, at the waterfall and fountain memorial, I was aware of how comforting my warm tears felt against my cool face as I remembered my father. I was so proud of him for having dedicated his life to being a good man. I moved slowly along the walkway constructed beneath a huge reflecting pool that spills over large pieces of granite from the Sierras and produces a continual roar of cascading water that soothes and silences all else in its range. At the end, it was the final wall—made of white marble—that gave me pause. It reads:

> No, no, we are not satisfied, and we will not be satisfied
> until justice rolls down like waters and righteousness like
> a mighty stream. March on Washington, 1963

An infectious rush of virtuous aspiration washed over me. What King had essentially figured out was how to break through the so-called "enemy," or wrong perception, that represented the barrier to mutual understanding and respect. While the enemy said, "You're less than! You're less than!" King replied, as if to say, I am not going to acquiesce to the negative ideas white people may hold about me. I am not. I am not. I am not. No, no. I will not adjust to that.

I could hear the sound of rushing water as it overrode nearly everything but the power and determination of King's voice resounding in my head: "We *are not* satisfied, and we *will not* be satisfied."

He broke through the wall of the enemy with his confident persistence. He simply refused to stop. No, not ever. He got so much energy from his conviction, and as I stood there, I did too. No, no, I am not going to adapt to what the patriarchy thinks of me. No matter what they say about me. The lives of Gandhi and King were continually threatened or under attack, yet they inspired so much energy, so much life. Even the word virtue, which they both embodied so skillfully, is related to the qualities of virility, or potency, or power. It was an internal force of love that impacted the planet.

IN HER WORK with the personality typology system called the Enneagram, Helen Palmer writes about how, when we transform a feature of the personality called a passion or a vice into its corresponding virtue, we experience a powerful energy. This is akin to the volcanic feeling I had when I got a glimpse of how to transform internal misogyny into its commensurate virtue of *feminine joy* by countering the internal critic or "enemy." When I let go of the hatred of the feminine, I glean all the aspects of the feminine that have been lost, like receiving a vitamin that I have been deficient in for quite some time.

King's recipe for continued righteous action inspired me to go deeper. In fact (to borrow vocabulary from the Enneagram system), it was a verbalization of the virtue that corresponded to my vice of disengagement. I could use this recipe for love to transform the disconnected "good girl," or the inoffensive kitten-like ego structure, into an engaged, fearless woman who would not stop until righteousness reigned for women.

When I begin to live my life with virtue, I gain the energy of this mighty stream. I embody the energy of the water. And that's why it feels generative and regenerative for me—I will not stop! I will not stop! I will not!

If it is truly virtuous,
Don't cease following your longing—ever,
Until the love overflows.

WAKING UP APHRODITE

*I have learned over the years that when one's mind is
made up, this diminishes fear; knowing what must be
done does away with fear.*

ROSA PARKS

Having an intellectual understanding of how to speak to
my internal misogynist and then actually practicing that
understanding were two very different things. One day, I
decided to sit down and write a script about just how I would address
my internal misogynist. I knew that I couldn't use shame, humiliation,
or fear tactics. No, I could not talk to it in the same way that it spoke
to me. Rather, I needed to speak with heart and truth. I needed to be
clear, very clear, and to continue to be clear, until this dangerous part
inside me had changed its tune. I created a three-part intervention.

First, I wanted to acknowledge the good intentions of my internal
misogynist. I like to think of this as joining with the resistance,
flowing with it. So when my dragon would start up with its old, outdated
song and dance, I would say something like, "Hey, it's me, Susie. I
hear you talking to me. And I can see that when you speak to me in
that way, you're trying to help me survive. So far, you've been pretty
successful. Thank you for that."

Second, I wanted to say what I needed then, which was to become
visible. I'd state my truth: "I don't want to be afraid of you anymore.
I don't want to just survive; I want to thrive. I want to feel a sense of

self-esteem and the rightful pride of being a woman. So when you speak to me, I need you to say positive things to me."

Third, I wanted to set a boundary generated from truth and heart—and this had to be done without any shame. "If and when you speak negatively to me, I will remind you that you need to say something positive instead, and that there is a boundary and a consequence to your behavior if you do not."

I could almost hear the dragon say, "And what if I don't?"

"Well, you're inside my body, and I'm navigating this ship. So if you refuse to stop, I'll simply refuse to allow space in my body and mind for this internal dialogue, and we can revisit it later, together."

Now I had my script, and it was time to put it into action. Over many days following my creation of this intervention, I disciplined myself to use the script to talk to the misogynistic self inside me.

AT FIRST, I was amazed at how empowered I felt knowing I could change this dragon. I had the power to change the ideas and feelings I'd allowed it to serve up to me. I had the ability to change the most dangerous part of my inner self. But it took time. That dragon had been expertly trained, mainly by my own observations of the culture I experienced as a young girl growing up. Any time I grew discouraged, which was very often after a while, in an effort to keep myself on track, I'd recall the sound of water flowing from my own proverbial fountain; I would find the energy to say King's words again and again and again:

> No, no, we . . . will not be satisfied until justice rolls down
> like waters and righteousness like a mighty stream.

Slowly, I started feeling better—more creative, and I was doing a better job of protecting myself. With time, I was able to say with more ease and skill what was on my mind. I had more courage to share my intuition. By refusing to adjust to a culture that wasn't good for me, I began to create my own. The more I did this, the less I would unconsciously adjust to misogyny, both internally and externally, and the more courage I would gain to say what I thought. Little did I know how much better my life would be.

My teaching classes grew better and better, and one day I was just stunned by something a student expressed. This particular class was during my favorite time, afternoon, and in my favorite building, art and science, which housed a display of photographic portraits of my peace-activist heroes—Alice Walker, Jimmy Carter, Mother Theresa, and many more. I started off our first meeting with my usual introduction and included a bit of my résumé, something that represented that very-needed element in any teaching situation: credibility.

I told them, "I've worked as a therapist with various populations including victims and perpetrators of domestic violence, emotionally disabled persons, adolescents, and others. I'm a trained mediator and also a trainer of mediators. I also use and teach the Enneagram. I teach in universities and have also worked in the corporate world, in employee-assistance programs and also as a relationship consultant in large organizations. Before beginning my private practice, I worked for a time as a therapist for the US Postal Service."

And always, after I'd rattled on a bit more about the salient portions of my résumé, someone would say, as if on cue, "Post office? You were a therapist in a post office, where they go postal?"

"Yes," I'd smile with a wink, and I'd tell them, "I did have a postal worker or two who'd say, 'Should I leave my gun at the door?'" The class laughed, and then I added, "Despite popular belief, there *are* actually some folks with a great sense of humor, not to mention some amazing people, known to lurk about the halls of post offices."

It was then that the student said, "When I found out I got into this class, I did a cartwheel." I was dumbfounded. She continued, "Another student said that this class changed her life. She said you got her to use her internal experience as a way to understand a case and then generalize, or expand, that experience to apply it to everything." This student was so animated while she succinctly summed up the psychotherapeutic relationship. "I want to learn that," she said, in a distinct tone.

Even though I was aware of the popularity of my class, I wasn't prepared for all this. Then another student told me that the students refer to me as an "icon." Wow. They were lovely, sincere students who were there with a clear motivation to learn. I'd forgotten just how inspiring they were.

The sky was clear, and, as I walked to my car in the late afternoon sunlight, I noticed that the pavement had turned to a smooth, almost ivory hue. As I stuck the key into the door lock, I considered the young women's unfettered delight. *A cartwheel?*

PEOPLE BEGAN ASKING me to give talks and lead groups. What inspired me was that my strengths, opinions, visions, and insights didn't just suddenly appear out of nowhere; these gifts had been with me all along, but I'd never before felt safe enough to allow them to emerge naturally. As I kept my dragon in check, with my divine feminine mystic internalized, I felt safe to say my piece and to offer whatever healing I could for those who asked. Because I no longer had an internal, ever-present threat inside me, I began to experience the beauty of allowing my individuality to come into view. I began to gather the fruits of this work.

I remember a quote a friend once shared with me, and, although she wasn't able to recall its source, she told me she thought an artist had said, "That will be the day when a painting cures a toothache." This quote stirred me, and I told her so. It helped me recall research I'd encountered that said that the most important factor in bringing healing to a client—more so than the theories used or even the interventions that they employed—was, quite simply, *the presence* of the therapist.

I recalled the day, now long ago, when I stood at the base of Mt. Everest and asked her, Chomolungma, what I should do with my life.

It was women and leadership that I'd heard when I asked, and yet I had rejected it. Why? I couldn't accept it *because* I had really wanted to do just that with my life and work.

Even though I'd received an award from Santa Clara University in recognition of my outstanding leadership, I couldn't begin to imagine such a thing as me working in the arena of women and leadership ever coming to pass, for the very simple reason that, deep down, I had really wanted it. Interestingly enough, this reaction is characteristic of the "bright shadow," the vision that held all of the positive aspects of me that I'd felt I could not claim. No wonder I rejected it.

Without owning control over my dragon, it continued to hold the treasure, the pearl that lay confiscated in its claw, the precious thing deep within me that I hadn't felt safe enough to reveal. But as I continued to build internal safety, I felt I could touch my bright shadow and act in support of its emergence. Inadvertently and paradoxically, my dragon was leading me to my goddess. It was through my weakness—my vulnerablity—that I was beginning to defeat the enemy.

> *How could we forget those ancient myths that stand*
> *at the beginning of all races, the myths about*
> *dragons that at the last moment are transformed*
> *into princesses? Perhaps all the dragons in our lives*
> *are princesses who are only waiting to see us act, just*
> *once, with beauty and courage. Perhaps everything*
> *that frightens us is, in its deepest essence, something*
> *helpless that wants our love.*
>
> RAINER MARIA RILKE

MATTER IN MOTION

Magic is the art of changing consciousness at will.
STARHAWK

THE DREAM

My father woke up with a terrified look on his face. He'd been asleep in his living room chair, which made a muffled scrape against the floor when he'd moved. He uttered a few words that I couldn't fully make out, but they carried the feeling of fear.

"Dad," I said, setting aside my laundry, "are you okay?"

"I had a nightmare."

"It seems like it. You look disturbed."

"I was trying to get to the wedding, but I couldn't make it there."

The whites of his eyes were prominent as he shifted again in the chair. He looked unusually unsettled.

"Can you say more of what was it about?" I asked, trying not to sound too much like a therapist.

"Well, I was trying to get to this wedding, and it was really important that I get there, and I couldn't. And I went to pick someone up at a house, and I was late."

"Why do you think it was important to get to this wedding?" I spoke slowly, quietly. I was trying not to disturb the trance-like recall of his nightmare.

"I don't know, but it was really frustrating because I knew—I just knew—that I needed to get to that wedding. And I couldn't."

I WATCHED HIM move again as he looked around, as though he were reminding himself that he was no longer in the dream. Then he arose and made some breakfast, and the nightmare became less of a focus.

But I was left with it. On my way down to the laundry room, I had questions. Why was it so important that he get to that wedding?

CALLED

*We are volcanoes. When we women offer our
experience as our truth, as human truth, all the
maps change. There are new mountains.*

URSULA K. LE GUIN

I had rented a small apartment with views of a fountain and pond
just across from the leasing office. Moffett Field and the San
Francisco Bay wetlands were just across the freeway, which is why
a pair of ducks often found it convenient to nestle in the rain gutter
above my front door. Occasionally I could see their beaks, or an eye
looking sideways, as I maneuvered my keys.

Rita Mae Brown was a cat I had inherited from my friend Pat
after she'd gotten a new dog, and the two didn't get along. Everyone
in my apartment complex knew Rita Mae because she looked like a
big, beautiful, fat penguin and had a boundary-defying personality. In
fact, my Italian friend used to hear her bellow for attention when we
talked on Skype, and he'd say "Ise dat dee peng wen?"

Yup, this was the place for strong women. It was a place where
I could put *me* out there, just like Rita Mae. And it was one where I
could take time to revisit old things I'd literally and metaphorically
kept in storage: my books, my ceramic dragons, my paintings, my
silverware, and my favorite colors. I'd forgotten what it was like to
create my own atmosphere. It was like having some good tea at the
right temperature—with the right stuff in it, like some honey—and

all ready to drink from a pretty cup. It was my sanctuary after my last breakup. And, besides their reputation as safe or sacred places, sanctuaries are often places where great events catalyze.

MY MOTHER CALLED. When the phone rang, I was at home mentoring a young woman who had just joined the staff at a domestic violence agency where I worked. Normally I wouldn't answer the phone in a situation like this, but we thought it was a consulting therapist returning our phone call, so I picked up and, to my surprise, my mother greeted me with a voice that sounded strangely stressed out.

"Sus," she said in an unusually low tone, "your father is really upset with me."

I couldn't get off the phone now that I had picked it up, and I was also caught by the fear in her voice. My intern waited silently.

"Your Aunt Bunny and I have been planning a party for my seventieth birthday," she went on, sounding exasperated, "and your father found out and got really, really mad. He said I should have told him."

"Okay," I said, not totally putting it together.

"And he told me I'd betrayed the marriage," she said, forlorn.

Silence. I looked at the young woman who was sitting next to me, politely waiting for me to conclude the call.

"Mom, let me call you back. I'm in the middle of something."

As I hung up the phone, the only thought running through my mind was, "Seriously?" After the young woman and I had concluded our meeting, I called my mom back. Teacups were still on the table, and Rita Mae had spread her twenty pounds across most of the couch.

My father answered.

"I was calling to talk to Mom. Would you tell me what is going on?" I said.

"I'm really mad at your mother. Your mother has betrayed the marriage," my father blurted out, and I continued listening, in shock.

"They didn't involve me in the party planning. I live in this house, and they didn't involve me."

"Excuse me?" I responded, in disbelief.

"Your aunt is planning a party at our house, and your mother didn't tell me, and I think it's just terrible." His voice had that authoritative, shaming sound, like when someone is found breaking a rule. I squinted out the window, braced myself, and put on my therapist's hat to play it back to him.

"What I hear you saying, Dad, is that you're upset at Mom for not telling you about the party?"

"Yes!" he said vehemently. "Your mother has betrayed the marriage."

"You feel betrayed?"

"Yes!"

There was a decided silence.

I couldn't believe it. Betray the marriage? Over planning a party? I felt my eyes roll. I wanted to just scream out over the phone, Come on! Are you serious? You must be joking! It's a frickin' party! And it's months away!

Plus, if I were my mother, I probably wouldn't include him in party planning, either, because I wouldn't think he'd want to plan a party. I couldn't recall him ever having planned a party.

I tried to hide the stress in my voice.

"Dad" I said evenly, "do you feel like I heard you?"

"Yes."

"Do you want to know what I think?" I said. I felt *so* prepared.

"Okay," he said.

"I am sorry, Dad, but I have no mercy for you. Ever since I've known you, I've never seen you plan a party for Mom, ever."

Bad attempt. Never use an evidence stance with an attorney—and especially not if the attorney happens to be your father.

"Well, I planned her sixty-fifth," he said.

"I was in Asia, so I didn't witness that." I said. "But why do you see *this* as betrayal? The birthday party is more than three months away."

And only one birthday, I thought, in how many years? I couldn't shake how ridiculous this entire conversation felt. Then my dad used one of his old lawyer tricks, which was to discredit the witness, although in this case—as in many over the years that I'd been his daughter—the witness he was attempting to discredit was me.

"Well you and I obviously have different views on marriage," he said.

It was an attack. Because I had been divorced, and since I had failed with marriage myself, I had no leg to stand on. With my response dismissed in these strange, metaphorical courtrooms he often conjured up, all I could say was, "So now you're attacking me, Dad?"

"Your mother is way out of line."

"Enough, Dad. Enough," I said tearfully. "I've heard enough of you criticizing mother. And I don't want to hear it any more."

With that, I hung up. I hung up, I hung up: I—hung—up, which meant I banged the receiver over and over against its cradle. It was an old phone, from the seventies, with a shiny orange plastic finish, and, in this case, the sound of plastic striking against plastic multiple times was deeply satisfying. I wasn't actually angry, but the intensity of my life force coursing through my veins was palpable, and it expressed itself in the repeated slamming.

I stared at the silent phone and, even after the fact, thought to myself: I can hang up now. The irony was that he had given me this very phone, along with a separate phone iine, when I was fifteen, so that I could be "more independent."

Suddenly, I became aware that I'd never hung up on my father before this. My mother—yes, but not him. I can do this, I thought. I felt a rush of elation and anger at the same time. I was so mad and empowered that I was beginning to wonder if I should be afraid that I wasn't afraid.

I paced around the room, raised my hands up in the air, and questioned myself on what to do. Then I sat at my laptop, and within ten minutes, which felt more like thirty seconds, I wrote him an email. This was not an agonizing, mulled-over, "oh-what-should-I-say," three-day kind of event—no, I was going to send that sucker immediately.

But then I paused over the send button and considered that maybe it was best to have someone look at it first. So I called my friend and confidant Daniel Potter because he is a great editor. And a guy is perfect for this, I thought. He read it, edited it a little here and there, and then he sent it back with a note of encouragement that felt like a campaign:

"Remember that Native American war cry, Sus," he wrote, "Today is a good day to die!"

What a way to put it, I thought. I looked at the final note, cc'd my mother, and then hit that tremendous send button. Here it is:

Subject: Apology and Thoughts

Dad,

I am sorry I hung up on you. That was rude of me. I should have told you I needed time out to think and deal with my own emotions rather than disrespect you. For that I apologize. I do love you. And it is because of this that I feel obliged to tell you what I think.

I think for you to see this as a betrayal in your marriage is unimaginably inappropriate. The party is three months away, which is exceedingly adequate notice, and the fact that you are upset at not being consulted from the beginning is just not a viable one.

To see this as betrayal makes a mockery of the word and blows the whole situation so far out of proportion that I am left at a complete loss to explain it. You yourself have betrayed your marriage more times than I can remember, by humiliating your wife in front of everyone, for ages. In my experience, your wife has bent way over backwards, contorted herself, and put you first, even in front of her own children, to make you happy. To put this insubstantial "lapse" in communication into a category such as betrayal is not only misogynistic, it is indicative of your abusive and insensitive behavior toward women in general, which I observed throughout my childhood.

You have been mean-spirited and angry with her for long enough! You have no further grounds to ever get mad at Mother again, after all she has done for you—just think about it. And if she ever does anything that hurts or bothers you, then you and your marriage would be well served to check with her first, to find out what causes you might have contributed as to her behaving that way. I would recommend you stop being so self-centered and start seeing how you can help women instead of criticizing them—try starting with your wife—if you truly wish to have a happier marriage and a happier life.

I know that this will be hard for you to hear and that in order to address this blind spot in your perception, you will have to take this in with sincere humility. As your daughter, I urge you to please take these words to heart. In the future, I will not support you in doing any more of your shaming toward women or anyone, so if you call me for that, I will not oblige. And if you truly meant what you said at Christmas,* then you will take this email to heart, as a signal from a loving daughter, to stop acting as a hater of women and find out how to start becoming an advocate for your wife's sex and mine!

Susie

*He had told my mother and me that he loved us above all.

SO THAT DAY I was left to imagine how I would live without my inheritance. I found myself pacing back and forth in my apartment. The phone rang mid-afternoon.

"Hi, Su Su. I need to talk to you about some mediation training dates." It was my mother. She sounded as if she hadn't received her copy of my email.

"Did you hear what happened with Dad?"

"Yes, he was quite surprised at your response," she reported cautiously, with an edge in her voice, as if to say she was also surprised, which seemed odd, since my response was in support of "her side."

"Did you get my email?" I asked proudly.

"No. What email?"

"Well, I sent you a copy. Shall I read it to you?" I enunciated slowly, to help bring her into focus for something important.

She consented with a "sure," but did so with a distracted air that added to my sense of urgency and the refined clarity I'd reached about my father's initial reaction to her.

I read the email to her somewhat quickly. My stomach shook the whole time. As I moved through the sentences, I began to take in the gravity of the message and realized that unless women—including my mother, in this case—were awake to the reality of the situation, they could be just as dangerous in their own misogyny as men were in theirs if they aligned with the misogynistic behavior directed against the one trying to help. When I finished reading, I let the last words hang. The other end of the line was silent. It was a moment so pregnant that I could almost hear it, as if it were a seedling popping up from this new terrain of freedom.

"Wow!" she exclaimed, as though she'd heard a resoundingly clear note emerge from a symphony of truth. Forty years of practice and Susie had finally achieved perfect pitch.

"I had no idea," she added.

Silence fell again.

Then she went on.

"You are dead-on, Susie. My first response to your father's reaction was to feel guilty, but you are right on. Wow!"

I could hear a renewed clarity emerge in the voice that had belonged to her long ago but had since been lost—until now. It was like a seemingly familiar but new friend you'd never met in this life—until just now.

"Wow! I never considered this," she said. "You are really right," she said again. I think she was blown away. I know she felt released.

For how long had I wanted to say this to my father, in this way? How much preparation had I done to get to this point? Was this finally the freedom from the shame that had so haunted both my mother and me all these years? My dad replied the next day, with this email:

Re: Thoughts and Apologies

Susie:

Thank you for sharing your feelings with me, with regards to my conduct over the years. It is not often that people will risk sharing their true feelings. I feel blessed.

I agree with everything you have observed. I have no excuses and accept your criticism as being valid. I feel badly about your experiencing this over the years and for this I apologize.

As for what I said at Christmastime, I spoke from my heart and that is all I can say.

I too love you and I look forward to our continuing relationship.

Love, Dad

Now it was my turn to say wow. What do I do when my dreams

come true? When I finally feel heard from the one man in my life that never seemed to hear me? The one who always had an argument— evidence, reasoning for why I was wrong?

I wrote him back with the truth.

> *Thanks, Dad. I really appreciate your response. It means more to me than you can know.*
>
> *Love,*
>
> *Sus*

A COUPLE DAYS later, which turned out to be Valentine's Day, my dad sent me beautiful white hydrangeas in an exquisite Chinese pot. I still have the pot, and it now holds an aloe vera plant.

He told me years later that my mother was the one who intervened that day and got him to do something different from what he'd planned.

"When I got your email, I felt defensive and wanted to write back about all of the good I had done for you. But your mother said, 'Now Jim, your daughter has put herself on the line. She has risked everything to say this to you. You might want to think differently about your response.'"

Somehow, my mother had connected, and I believe that what she did was catalyzed by my own internal work with the intervention inspired by the story of what Anansel had done with the enemy. My mother was responding to the strength I'd built inside. She expressed my vulnerability and my courage so that my father could see that this was a heartfelt plea, not an attack.

My email had awakened her to her own internal power, so that she could be gentle and firm with my dad. He said it was at that moment that he got it, so to speak—that since I'd been willing to risk, he was able to have compassion and look at the situation differently. I think this might be at the core—that core undefended place that speaks out and affects others so deeply. Perhaps that is what King and Gandhi had—that undefended, fierce love for others, as well as a love for all the parts of themselves.

The powerful clarity of my declaration, my mother's interventions, and my father's ability to fully hear and respond all continue to remind me of the beauty of the path of the labyrinth, a path of being in the same place at different times, of seeing the same dragons again and again, yet seemingly meandering off course at times. And then one day—boom!—to hit the send button, to hit that central note, and, having discovered oneself, to return to the center, to empower others to do the same.

Those around you feel safe
When you've taken responsibility
For yourself.

RIPPLES

Each time a man stands up for an ideal, or acts to improve the lot
of others, or strikes out against injustice, he sends forth a tiny ripple
of hope, and crossing each other from a million different centers of
energy and daring, those ripples build a current which can sweep
down the mightiest walls of oppression and resistance.

ROBERT F. KENNEDY

To rainy weeks passed. I went on in my world and turned my mind to other things. I didn't realize the full impact of my email until a couple of weeks later, when my parents were in Palm Springs.

Palm Springs is my mother's hometown and now a place of respite for her with old friends. When she was young there, it was a conservative community where old blue blood families lived a life of golf and thank-you notes. It's far removed from the lifestyle my parents have in northern California, which is a liberal, spiritual, progressive world filled with ceremonies, political marches, and ideals of saving the world. In my mother's former world of Palm Springs, people have short, cute names like Minnie and Tad, and I have early memories of many of those folks. For me, hearing their voices brings back poolside conversations, the sound of tennis balls hitting pavement, and traditional Republican politics.

"Su Su!" my mom announced breathlessly as I answered the phone. "Honey, you would not believe this. Your father is so different. He's slipped a few times, but since your email, he's been very aware of his behavior. He has been talking about it with his friends. I've had long talks about it with my female friends, too. They were all so interested, and they wondered how this might affect their lives."

For my entire life, I had tried to get my father to treat my mother better. From the way he always put her down to the way he corrected her, it was as though he thought she couldn't do anything right. It was hard for me, and all of their friends watched it happen as well.

I would yell and say, "Stop doing that! Stop saying that!" And yet, it never had any impact. So for my mother to call and say, "He's so different," I was agog: Palm Springs, Smoke Tree Ranch, and their conservative friends discussing that email? No way. I mean, my parents' friends were nice people, and they had always been great friends to my parents, but I had never considered them the "work-on-relationship" type. In fact, in the seventies, they were the ones who used to tease my parents about these kinds of things. So much for stereotypes.

"Would you believe my friends here are thinking about this!" my mother exclaimed.

When our call ended, I found myself in a kind of trance.

TWO WEEKS LATER, I received another phone call from my mom. She and Dad were back in town and wanted to come over.

"Honey, your father and I want to bicycle to your place and talk with you. Is that ok?"

I looked around at my apartment and figured it could look better by the time they arrived.

"Uh, sure. When?"

"Well, we'd be leaving our house in a few minutes."

I was intrigued and surprised. They'd only rarely come to the places where I'd lived. I don't even know if they'd visited my apartment here yet—maybe once.

"OK," I said, smiling, "I'll be ready for you." I hung up the phone and scanned my apartment again. It was raining that day. And to bike over? How odd. At the time I lived about five or six miles from their home in Palo Alto.

Sure enough, my parents showed up on their bicycles wearing matching yellow rain slickers, black lycra outfits, and helmets and gloves— basically, the works. They came up the stairs, breathing heavily but with excitement in their eyes.

"Would you like some tea?" I asked, having been well trained by my grandmother and by my Jane Austen novels.

"Do you have some of that tea and honey from Damanhur?" my mother asked. Of course, I did. She was always enchanted with the objects I brought home from exotic places. It was fun to make her happy.

The rain continued to pour, and my apartment was great then— especially cozy—and the fountain just beyond my windows added to the effect, as if it were my own private little grotto in Mountain View.

My parents sat down and started talking about Bill so-and-so and Bob so-and-so and all of these men who wanted to know about the email. They all wanted to know the same thing: did their wives and daughters feel the same way?

"I hope you don't mind, Susie, but I shared our email exchange with some of my friends," my dad said. I couldn't summon the faces that went with the names, but I got a picture of the desert walks, the khaki pants, and the golf shirts.

"Great!" I said in support, while serving them tea. The steam that rose from the cups was another comforting complement to the rain.

"One of my friend's responses was, 'I am worse than you!'" My father laughed like he used to when we were kids.

"He was wondering if his daughters and wife had the same experiences you did, Sus. And I've had other conversations," he explained.

He went on excitedly about all that he'd been confessing and learning. It was breathtaking to watch him open this emotional window with such Aikido-style strength. Not only was he learning about misogyny, but he was also doing it so well—with no resistance.

He went on and on and then finally sat back and began to ask me questions about my life, while my mother relaxed in my old, down-stuffed French chair as she grinned and savored the honeyed tea. They had come home from their vacation empowered, and, like kids returning from summer camp, they wanted to share their experiences with me because I had been such a part of it all. My father asked me how I was doing after my recent breakup, and that was a new experience for me because, although I knew he cared for me, that subject was something I'd never thought was of interest to him.

"I've been struggling," I confessed, honestly. "It's been so much like my divorce—the fact that I'm having to deal with that sort of thing all over again, with such pain and discouragement."

He asked me specifically why I ever went out with the last guy because, he said, "I didn't like the way he assumed you should do everything the way *he* wanted."

"Well, Dad," I answered bluntly, "maybe you were looking in a mirror."

"Fair enough," he said with a laugh.

My mother looked pleasantly surprised yet remained quiet, as if being careful not to disturb the flow of the magnificent hour that was upon us.

I told him about a dream I'd had where he and my most recent ex-boyfriend were working on a project together, and how it had seemed to me that he and my father looked alike, with the same haircut and same eyes. I told him how they were both like a piece of stone that looked rough on the outside but was really jewel-like inside, and how I had observed that my ex was, in fact, a genius. The sad part was that, like my father, he pushed people away when he felt shame and then made them the vessel for his own shame. I also told my dad that, back then, neither of them could see the affect their behavior had on others—they could only catch glimpses of it—but that now, it seemed, he was really changing. It was a conversation I never dreamed I'd have with my father.

He listened intently, as though he had just learned a new language and could finally comprehend it when it was spoken to him. I found myself talking for quite a while, as my mother continued to listen and watch us. Then, after a while, they both just listened. It was certainly a new forum for me.

They stayed for three hours, and then my mother said they needed to go, but my dad countered that he didn't want to leave. I was blown away.

Then he astonished me again. He asked if he could present the email exchange to his men's group. Inspired by the religious organization we belonged to, they began meeting when I was in high school, some twenty years before.

The kind faces of those men came to mind, and some of their daughters' faces did, too. "Absolutely," I answered. "Share it with anyone." Why not, I thought.

A FEW DAYS later, I called about some other matter, and, as if approaching a checklist item, he said, "Susie, I've been meaning to call you."

I felt like I'd been waiting for a casting call from a director.

"I presented our email exchange to the men's group," he said. "They wanted to make sure I told you that they were really impressed with the email. They said it was like a laser beam had hit the point. And one gentleman in the group was so moved that he decided to write a letter of apology to his estranged daughter of fifteen years."

To say that this moved me was an understatement. I felt touched, as if by an angel. It seemed that her father now had some new insights about their estrangement.

And then these men began to write me letters. I remember getting a letter and reading it right before I got in the shower, and then, as the water began pouring down on me, I realized—Wow! I've finally found a way to be heard.

In a most beautiful handwritten note, the father of the estranged daughter wrote to me,

> *Dear Susie,*
>
> *Your generous, candid sharing of your insights into the emotional encounters with the men in your life has moved me to peek a little deeper into my own long-fortified cavern of misogyny and ignorance. And although I have pleaded*
>
> *in my letters to my daughter for reconciliation during the last fifteen years, it has been to protest my innocence from her accusation of physical abuse, with no admission to or addressing of the damage I inflicted emotionally. My unconscious anger toward women [which I had] directed to her precluded any loving father-daughter relationship.*
>
> *My wife and I both admit our ignorance then in failing to cope with her need. I am sure we could benefit from open talks now. But after these many years and no response from her, it is possibly "water under the bridge." However, Susie, thanks to you and Jim, I have sent another letter to her, admitting my guilt, including apology, and hoping for her forgiveness.*
>
> *Love (and gratitude),*

Incredibly, these men, most all of whom were born in the 1920s and 1930s, were asking themselves, "Am I a misogynist?" And it had never before really occurred to them. On some level, it became apparent that they wanted to understand this, so that they could then come to understand their wives and daughters. It was a heartfelt discovery that rippled on and on.

FOR THE NEXT few years, my father shared the email. And I shared it at talks and lectures. Women would approach me and say, "I want my father to change," and I'd always tell them, "I changed myself, and that is what affected my father." I could say it to my dad only because I was able to say it to myself. It's how you treat yourself inside that allows you to talk with authenticity and certainty to others.

I wonder if this is what Gandhi meant when he spoke of dealing with his own demons? Is it when I deal with my own demons that others often begin to deal with theirs? Was that the difference this time, as opposed to the 600 million other times I'd tried to reach my father? There was nothing like this feeling I had then—a happiness that was familiar, but from a memory I wasn't conscious of—an ancient sense of fulfillment that was only just beginning.

Receive those who,
At the expense of their own ego,
Step courageously
into the light.

VIRTUE

If you want to make peace, you don't talk to your friends.
You talk to your enemies.

MOSHE DAYAN

When I was in my mid-twenties, my dad was diagnosed with a heart condition, and I began to worry: what if something were to happen to him? Because of this, we started a tradition then of having lunch together every week. Over time, we stopped, but after our email exchange, he announced, "Let's start doing our lunches again." And so we did, almost twenty years later.

We would talk and talk and talk, mainly over sushi at Momoya's, in Mountain View. We had a few arguments here and there, but generally it was a forum to bring out what either of us was curious about. During these renewed lunch and eventual dinner dates, I received the parenting from my father that he had avoided when I was a kid.

Even in my forties, I could feel the kid inside me sigh in relief at finally having a father. When I was dating again, he would give me advice like, "Susie, I wouldn't go into all of the details about your divorce when you're on dates."

As my internal rift was healing with all these new interactions between my father and me, I had an insight. If this life is like a dream, and every aspect of the dream is a reflection, or display, of some aspect of the self, or one's own mind, then maybe we have this dream to make our own issues tangible and therefore easier to touch and address. Perhaps the internal is mirrored for us externally so we can have opportunities to see it and work on it. And when I worked on my own internal misogynistic rift, I found that I felt better, and others began to treat me differently.

The energy, or virtue, that came from this shadow confrontation with my father allowed for both of us to continue to be brave, ask questions, and relate in such a way that fear did not rule. My father, a man who had felt for so long that he could not parent his daughter, was now brave enough to aid in her healing.

After all these events occurred and my father had begun to work hard on accepting the feminine and treating women with respect, a normal yet amazing event presented itself. My brother's wife gave birth to a daughter, the first grandchild in the family.

My brother and his wife delivered a gift to my father and to his world—a relationship that gave substance to his new capacity for relating to the feminine—and so it was that he began a relationship with this little girl. When my father and his granddaughter met, they became instant best friends. My brother and his wife asked if he would take her for one day a week as she was growing up. So moved was he at their request that he stepped right into service, and he and his granddaughter did all sorts of activities together. I realized what a tremendous gift this was for my father, who, after all this work, got to be a part of this little girl's upbringing, this girl who simply adored him. He got to practice his new skills and be totally embraced and mutually loved in the process.

One day when she was seven, I was invited to hear something special at his retirement community. In front of all his friends, she sang him a very old, favorite song his family used to sing called "Sentimental Journey." While she sang, something hit me like a strong wind. It was an insight regarding the dream he'd had—that nightmare about the wedding he was struggling to get to.

I understood that, from his perspective as a heterosexual, the dream was about his journey to that place where the masculine and feminine could meet. And the terror he felt was about the fear of it not coming to pass in his lifetime. But now he had a place where he could meet his own feminine, on the inside. He had finally overcome that nightmare. And because of that, when his son eventually had a daughter, his first granddaughter, he had created a safe space for her to meet him and love him and feel safe. It was as though he'd been granted the gift of a do-over, a parenting do-over.

That's when it really came home to me that, once my father and I had accepted the challenges of the rift caused by misogyny, we both were able to transform the blocks that resulted from this ancient hatred, so that we could stand in this divine place of love. By opening to the intelligence of the feminine, the masculine was able to grow more skillful and, therefore, stronger.

My father, Jim, and his granddaughter 2006, California

Energy comes from freeing love.

RELEASE

The only thing that makes life possible is permanent,
intolerable uncertainty: not knowing what comes next.

URSULA K. LE GUIN

EXCHANGE

While driving from Arizona to Truckee, California, I received a call that my ex-husband had died. The news was totally unexpected, but the fact that I was on my way to where he had just died made it seem even more surreal. I didn't have any strong feelings about it at first, other than a sort of shock. But the drive afforded me many hours to think about all sorts of memories, to call everyone I knew, and to put myriad pieces of uncanny information together.

He died almost exactly thirteen years after the last time we'd spoken in person, in March of '98. I met him when I was thirteen, in March of '76, and, was married to him for thirteen years, from March of '85 to March of '98. When he died, in March of 2011, he was forty-nine. (I added the numbers: four plus nine equals thirteen—the numerology for his chronological age at death.)

While looking back at my dark night, I also discovered some old pictures of myself, where I was wearing my favorite shirt. I was surprised to see the shirt bore the number thirteen.

The more I thought about it, the more mysterious the number seemed. Thirteen, in the context of my new-age religious upbringing, was considered a mystical number. A song had even been written about it. It was part of a musical, and, as I chewed on the memories and attempted to recall the words, I realized I'd seen that musical when I was thirteen.

During my driving breaks en route to Truckee, I scoured Wikipedia and various websites in search of more information about the number. I wasn't surprised to learn that, in ancient cultures, thirteen was associated with the feminine because the lunar year—matching a typical menstrual cycle of twenty-eight days—generally consists of thirteen moons, each containing a twenty-eight-day moon cycle. But as with many other feminine associations, the number thirteen eventually became the number of the devil and was synonymous with being unlucky. Hmmmm.

I don't understand why this number was part of my relationship with Chuck or how I thought to put it together, but somehow I sensed that the pattern was telling me something.

Then the grief hit, and it caught me off guard. I wouldn't have thought it would've affected me so intensely, but when I learned that he'd died in the backseat of a car—alone—from a heart attack, I was deeply pained. I'd assumed that if Chuck died, I would wear the proverbial red dress to his funeral, but when it actually happened, I didn't feel that way.

I felt grief, which was surreal because the humiliation had cleared me of any discernible feelings for him for so many years. At the time I learned of his death, I didn't feel the same shame-ridden horror that I'd experienced earlier in our relationship; I had a sweet kind of grief. The sense of closeness that I'd shared with him was such that I worried about him even then, in his death. My grieving was far less painful than my dark-night journey had been, but it was grief, nonetheless.

WHILE I WAS driving again, just a few days after Chuck had died,

I heard a song from *Phantom of the Opera* playing over the radio. A beautiful male voice sang opening lines that went something like: No more talk of darkness, just forget these wide-eyed fears. I'm here right beside you, to hold you and to guide you. I felt high hearing the music, and then I felt Chuck's presence. I could actually see him. He wore his favorite red Hawaiian shirt and a pair of old checked shorts that made for a real mismatch. He had color in his cheeks, and he looked like he did when we first realized we wanted to marry.

Rather quickly then, many images came to me. One was of his mother's house in Santa Barbara, where we'd felt so ecstatic about each other. I prided myself on remembering, but I hadn't visited these places or memories in so long, and yet they were crystal clear. Suddenly, I felt a strong urge to tell someone to make sure they placed some of his ashes along the beach.

Then Chuck seemed to put his hand on my shoulder and transmit a deep love toward me, like an apology. He was sorry, which I could feel in my bones.

"It's okay," I communicated. "I got through it."

"It's not okay," he replied. "What I did was horrible, and now I'm truly sorry."

As I heard these words, I remembered a movie about a music instructor who was teaching one of his students that achieving excellence in playing music was not for the purpose of making money. It wasn't until after his teacher's death that the student understood the teacher's frustration with him for having decided to be a court composer. The instructor had taught him how to play so beautifully that the dead would come to hear him. This instructor had played the violin, and his wife, whose death was long before his, would appear at the sound of his playing. After gaining insight into this, the student was able to play music so beautifully that his teacher, who by that point was also deceased, would actually appear to him and confirm it.

As I continued my drive, I intuited that the song on the radio sounded so beautiful that Chuck was appearing before me. The song continued, and I mused upon the ironic and synchronistic serendipity that this piece of music was about: the ending of a dark night for the woman this male actor was singing to in *The Phantom of the Opera*. "No more talk of darkness," the voice sang, and here Chuck was, telling me the same thing.

THE NEXT DAY I went to see a friend. She knew Chuck only in a tangential way, but she was fully present to hear my story of his death and the experience I'd had in the car. My friends now show no surprise about me having these sorts of experiences, such as talking to the dead, but her surprise about his apology was fresh. We decided to walk on the beach, not far from her home. As I descended the cliff on the path to the sand, I was struck by the beauty of the day. The minute my foot pressed upon the sand, I heard the song at full volume in my head, and Chuck appeared again. I felt him ask, "Can I walk with you?" It felt odd, the realness of the request, and I paused to logically digest it and decipher if I was perhaps making it up.

I'd had a similar feeling when I knew the day that my grandmother was dying. I felt a sense of complete intimacy, and the left side of my brain relaxed. Moreover, I experienced too much clarity in the process for me to have been making up what transpired, so I settled with the idea this might be real. But I was still startled again when Chuck spoke as if to allay my fears and set his intentions. "I just want to walk with you and be with you on the beach," he told me. So we walked together, and I cried. In homage to him for appearing and for the energy, or source, that had evoked this healing meeting between the worlds, so to speak, I made shell and stone designs on the sand. I remembered a poster he'd had in high school. It featured a couple walking on a beach, and there was a poem at the base of the image.

When we married, Chuck said he realized the poster's importance in relation to his adolescent self and how he'd been looking for someone to walk with on the "beach of life." Then he concluded that I'd been the one he was searching for. And soon after his death, there we were, doing just that, walking on the beach. In retrospect, I felt like Aphrodite coming out of the water. It was the completion of Chuck's life and the reemergence of mine.

The love I felt pouring out of him then was a full-spectrum kind of love, a pure love that wasn't tied to marriage or drama. It was two beings realizing the beauty of this play we call "life"—the beauty of the struggle. It felt like the kind of love that might happen when you're done with the play or finished with a huge project and free to celebrate the success of it together—the unconditional love of the shared experience. That moment was like being in a theater's green room, the place where the actors and actresses relax and center themselves before going onto the stage. Here, we could evaluate the play itself and compare notes. That was the last time I had this sort of experience with Chuck, and I've felt complete about him ever since.

However, after that I literally felt haunted, in a good way though, and I was left with an intense desire to reach out to Chuck's widow, Carol. I was a bit scared, really, because I was uncertain about how I'd be received. So I wrote Carol a note and mailed it.

Dear Carol,

I must confess, this is a letter that I never imagined I'd be writing, but I've been thinking about it since the minute I received news of Charles's death. The thought won't leave me, so I've put fingers to keys.

As you may know, Charles (I should say Chuck because that's who he was then) and I ended very badly, and I suspect you watched him express his anger toward me, so you may see me mostly through his eyes and the eyes of those who considered my reactions unfair. So, if that is the case, I would conclude that, among other obvious reasons why this letter might be difficult for you, you might not want to hear from me. Despite that thought, I decided to write anyway, and I hope that is okay.

We've shared so many things from having been married to him, you and I. Weird, isn't it? I think about it this way: We shared Betty Kenny as a mother-in-law and an entire family of in-laws, and a flock of friends who are Yalies (maybe you went to Yale too, and I was alone in that culture shock . . .) Now this is the one that I found truly interesting: we shared three cats, I believe, or at least two, and, if things hadn't changed very much, you must have witnessed every possible derivation of their names: "Hopping," "Squirting," "Squeaking" . . . or "the Val," "Monster," or "The Beast," and, of course, "Hoodly Boodlies."

You and I share another connection, which is unrelated to Charles. I learned you were from Michigan; my father was raised in East Lansing and earned his undergraduate degree at Michigan State long, long ago. So many connections.

I am truly shocked and sorry to hear about your loss. It's hard to predict how someone will react to a death, and I have no idea how you are reacting, but I want you to know that my heart goes out to you. Grief and loss suck, no matter how you slice it. In past experiences, it's been like having my cells torn apart. I heard about the ceremony you had for Charles on Sunday night, March 27th. I think that is a most loving and compassionate act. It seems that he was able to reach his dreams in your presence—in his life with you—and that is a relief to me. In my opinion, he was lucky to have you in his life.

His death has thrown me for a loop. At my desk today I was reading the email about the service this weekend, and I looked at his birth date and just started weeping. I'm finding it a shock to my body despite all the processing and healing I've done over the years and the happy place that I've been in lately. My mind is filled with memories I hadn't let in, and now I have a desire to connect to those who knew him—us, and others. I never expected this. Thanks for reading this, if you have. If you want to communicate at some point, any point, please do. May the angels surround you with soft feathers.

Warmly,

Susie

CAROL WROTE BACK, and eventually we made plans to meet. But first was the memorial, which was overwhelming: While immersed in an auditorium with close to two thousand people, so large because Chuck was a public figure in the area, I saw all of Chuck's family—everyone I hadn't seen in thirteen years. Pictures of Chuck, a number of which I had taken, were projected onto a large screen, and selections of his music collection that I hadn't heard since I'd left home were playing. I watched a very formal, orchestrated service and realized that, since his parents were now dead, I was the person in the room who'd lived with him the longest, and yet there was no mention of me anywhere in the service, not even a word about the fact that he'd been married previously. Outside the auditorium, Carol was lovely, and as we shared a hug, she said softly, "We loved the same man."

Begin to cohere your story by noticing the synchronicities around you. The magic in them will remind you of your pilgrimage.

CHUCK'S PEARLS

We work on ourselves, then, in order to help others.
And we help others as a vehicle for working on ourselves.

RAM DASS and PAUL GORMAN

The morning I was supposed to meet Carol, I didn't allow enough time to find the one thing I wanted to give her—Chuck's baby pearls. They were something that his mother had given to me years ago, for my keeping. Despite seeing them a million times, I couldn't find them. I grabbed something else instead, something that was really precious to me, something that I had known, from the moment I'd received it, that it was meant for someone special. It was a white ceremonial silk scarf, a khata, that Tashi had given me, which had been blessed by the Dalai Lama himself. I combined it with some incense I had and threw myself into the car.

I drove the usual route to Marin. It was a stunning day. The redwoods and the sounds had been so much a part of my life when I lived there. I parked at The Depot, in Mill Valley, and felt oddly elated, so after I'd filled my meter, I filled an older couple's meter too, just as they pulled in.

As I stepped onto the patio, Carol recognized me, which was not what I'd expected, but in hindsight it made sense. We first met in a blur, at the memorial, but she'd seen pictures of me many times before that.

I'd assumed we'd have tea, but she looked prepared to just drop off the photo albums, which was the reason we were meeting. Without thinking, I blurted, "Shall we talk over tea?" She agreed.

After we'd settled ourselves at a patio table, I gave her the khata and some incense, and she seemed moved. I'd assumed she was familiar with khatas, yet it seemed as if she weren't.

"I was worried that if I had told you how many albums there were, you might not have come," she began. "There are ten albums."

I raised my eyebrows in amusement at my memory of Chuck and how he could put any scrapbooking expert to shame. He loved to chronicle his life.

"It doesn't surprise me in the least, even though I'd forgotten how many there were!" I said, laughing. I'd expected two, but I was excited just to have them then, regardless of the number. She looked at me with concern, and I told her not to worry at all. "I know he loved making those albums," I added, "and I'm so grateful that you reached out to me."

We talked about his passing, and I told her I had really grieved for him the Saturday after I'd first heard about his death. She looked eager to tell me, almost as if to say it'd been synchronistic, that that Saturday had been the day of his private funeral, when his close friends and family had gathered for a ceremony and his cremation. I had felt a longing on that Saturday. I'd had the inkling that something was happening then—perhaps it had been a sign from Chuck?

I looked at Carol with a concerned intent. "How did you survive that? How did you deal with the cremation?"

Then she divulged something wise and unexpected. She said it was like the times when she'd trim her cat's claws and say to them, "Honey this won't hurt—it's just dead skin." So, she told me that right before his body was to be cremated, she said to Chuck, "Don't worry honey, you will be okay. What will be burned is already dead, and it won't hurt you at all. You don't need to be afraid." It was at that point that I started to get a window into the special quality Carol had.

Then she told me about how she'd followed *The Tibetan Book of Living and Dying*. When Chuck's body arrived, she said, the funeral home staff was really accommodating because she'd basically camped out there, sitting with the body for about five days and reading to him from *The Tibetan Book of the Dead*. I got the impression that, to the best of her understanding, she had followed all the protocols in that ancient document.

I looked at her in astonishment because, on so many levels, everything she was saying had such meaning for me, and it was clear to me that it had been so for her as well. *The Tibetan Book of Living and Dying* had been a great help to me in gaining some understanding of the meaning of "bardo." Giving her the khata then brought it all together. How is it that Chuck had ended up with so much Buddhist support?

"The woman who gave me the khata is the niece of Sogyal Rinpoche, the author of the book," I finally told Carol. We looked at each other in what was an astonishing moment for me, at least, and I think it was for her as well. I wondered if maybe later I could also tell Carol that Tashi was the person who'd held a lantern of compassion for me throughout my dark night, to help me to see the way.

"He was my prince," she professed, and I felt her conviction.

What a lucky guy he was to have found this woman to love him and also help him die well. I was moved beyond words that Carol had done this incredibly loving thing for Charles.

As I looked at her again, I felt grief. "You must be going through a lot."

"It's been tough as of late," she confessed quietly, which sounded like it might've been the anxiety phase of her grief, and then she added, "I don't know if I'm over it yet." As an old hand at grief, I didn't have the heart to tell her that, in all likelihood, it had only just begun.

She asked how I was doing, and I said that I'd grieved at length about him long ago. In comparison then, I expected that my grief over his death would likely last just a few months.

Carol said that, as she looked through the photo albums, she could see that Chuck and I must have loved each other very much, and that, from the pictures, we looked like we were very close. I did love him, too, I thought. The pain I'd gone through since those photographs were taken, and the recent healing as well, had made me feel like one of those old travelers, laughing at my younger self and all the drama of my life then. For a moment, I savored this wistful emotion.

"The marriage and its ending must have been hard for you," she said. I looked up at her and saw a familiar expression in her eyes. It reminded me of the steady, even eye gaze of Ani Karen. I was unprepared for Carol's compassion, too. It was coming from such an unexpected quarter—my ex-husband's wife?

I considered her for a second and wondered if she would ever know just how hard my own experience with him had been.

"It was a dark night, but I'm all the better for it now," I said and smiled.

ALL THE WORK I had done in regard to all those difficult times gave me the ultimate gift. People are beautiful mirrors.

I understand that, in a deep sense, my ideas about who my father is today are reflections of the father I've created inside. He is responsive, and he cares and stands up for me. It's the interior work that reveals the magic. The inside is what's real.

When you are face-to-face with misogyny,
Transform it for the future, and
Remember: you are in good company.

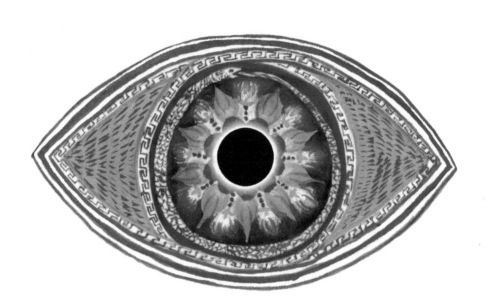

A MOST UNEXPECTED PLACE

Of what is the body made? It is made of emptiness and rhythm.
At the ultimate heart of the body, at the heart of the world,
there is no solidity . . . there is only the dance.

GEORGE LEONARD

After our meeting, Carol and I had a lovely email exchange.
She wrote me this final note:

Hi Susie,

After I sent that email I realized that I had forgotten to thank you for
the lovely, blessed khata and the incense. I've already had occasion
to impress friends by wearing the khata, and when I'm not wearing
it, I drape it over a framed group of photos of my family (Charles
and all the animals), to ensure their happiness and protection.
My deepest thanks for that very thoughtful gift,

Carol

What began so long ago as Tashi's gift to me was now something
that I could give to this unexpected and unique human being, a woman
who would effect healing in me with her compassion and understanding
of the challenges I had faced in my marriage to Chuck, and who had
the intuition and fortitude to know how to help him in his death by
reciting *The Tibetan Book of the Dead.* Even more intriguing was that

many years earlier, Chuck had given me that turquoise wool scarf, which, on my first trip to Tibet, I'd given to Tashi. Unbeknownst to me until much later, that scarf was very significant to Tashi, just as Carol's khata was now used to honor her family's picture.

It was an exchange, full circle. Tashi had shown me a way, a meandering way, to work through the bardo of my life, and the many bardos within that.

She gave me a map to navigate the perils of remaining compassionate during even the most transgressive moments of my life. After my experience on the beach with Chuck, I had felt a total and complete sense of love, and there seemed to be one word to capture that feeling—divine.

Exchange is relationship. We learn from each other and develop ourselves. Later, through Carol, I learned that Chuck's political work in support of the environment is still bearing substantial fruit today. This was literally heartwarming: he started that work with me because I was so passionate about it. I can see now why raising a child takes a village because it took a village to heal me, and I got to be part of the village that inspired Chuck.

When I share the story about the pivotal exchange I had with my father, I often hear, "Can I have a copy of that email you sent to your father? I want my father to change." I remember the feeling of wanting my father to change, and I can totally relate. But I have to share with them that it's not about changing your father; it's about the impact that you have on your father and others when you change yourself. As I watched my father over the last thirteen years of his life, he mirrored the father I had created inside. He was responsive, and he cared for and stood up for me. People are just mirrors.

This idea relates to a powerful scene in the movie *The Matrix*, where a young child holds up a spoon and, after staring at it intently, seemingly bends the spoon upon command, without touching it. The main character, Neo, is astonished by this feat, and the child replies,

"Do not try and bend the spoon. That's impossible. Instead, only try to realize the truth." Neo says, "What truth?" The child answers, "There is no spoon." Neo replies, "There is no spoon?" And the child tells Neo, "Then you'll see that it is not the spoon that bends; it is only our self."

I RECALLED THE time when I'd visited Tashi just before her untimely passing. I walked through the streets of Lhasa to meet her, as I'd done so many times before. My impression from the rooftop country of Tibet is that experiencing clarity is so accessible there, with the proximity of the intense sunlight and the thin air. The elements evoked feelings of purity and love inside me as I walked.

I waved hello to my usual friends along the way to Tashi's house, to the second floor of that same building—the place where I'd first met her, all those years before. Her apartment had hardly changed over the years. Everyone on the floor shared a toilet, and those were ancient, to say the least. The environment was so far from what I'd had in my upbringing, yet this one was so close to my heart. Every tattered doorway, every tile was precious to me because it held so much history, so much pain, and so many reminders of enlightenment.

Tashi sat on a carpet-draped sleeping bench, and we faced each other. I looked at this woman, loved by so many Westerners who had come through, and marveled how her life had been a teaching for me. The hardships she faced were so far beyond anything I could imagine.

"Thank you for telling me your story," I said. "It is so useful to know because the world is changing so fast, and it is all so precarious: my generation and the younger ones will be facing vast challenges. It's good to hear from those who've not only survived such difficulties but have come through them with their heart intact."

"You can tell people my story, if you think it would be helpful," she said. Her husband came in then and nodded hello. I was in awe of them both. He went into another area of the apartment, and Tashi and I had more time together.

She gestured to me, as though she wanted to show me something. I was drinking milk tea, which was my sweet, warm substance of choice in Tibet, and I put down my cup and leaned close, toward her. She dug into the folds of her shirt and pulled at a string hanging around her neck. Up came a piece of turquoise, and when it came into full view, she said, "This is it."

She held it up for several moments before I realized what she was talking about. And then I remembered: it had been her first husband's earring—*his* turquoise earring. Tashi had been able to hang on to that piece of turquoise through it all—when she came close to starving, when she was beaten, and all of the other horrors that I could speculate she must've endured. She still had his earring on a string around her neck. The scarf, of course . . . the scarf. Now I thought I'd begun to more fully understand why she'd kept and worn that turquoise-colored scarf ever since I'd presented it to her.

"That's amazing," I mumbled, "really amazing. Wow! It's his earring?" I felt dizzy and breathless—dumbfounded. The immense significance of this small stone was pounding itself into my senses all at once; it was her story—the power of love, how truly powerful truth and compassion are when practiced together, inseparably—and it was all conveyed by the potency of this one small, blessed stone that I got to experience before she left the world.

AND THEN, IT was time to go. In our final moment, we touched foreheads to say goodbye—for this life—in that beloved room above the family restaurant. It was a full circle: the beginning was the end. The layers were dancing together. We were all totally connected. And by following the meandering path, I was eventually led to the center, that place so far inside me that I'm outside my self, that divine place where the way out is the way in—the labyrinth of my life.

EPILOGUE

Steve Omohundro called Susie late in the summer of 2005 to see if she was interested in meeting this guy Brad he knew. After hearing that he was a Tibetan Buddhist, spoke Nepali, and knew the Enneagram, she said with trepidation, "Bring him to next week's dialogue group."

Steve, very wisely, did not mention this conversation to Brad. After five weeks of coming to dialogue, Brad made his move. He hid in Susie's bathroom near the end of the meeting held in her home and waited for everyone else to leave. He emerged only to realize that after ten minutes of waiting he had neglected to think of anything to say. Panicked, he glanced up and managed to see some unidentifiable objects atop a bookcase, pointed there, and asked her what they were.

Susie said with delight, "Those are my dragons!"

Ask, and it shall be given you;
Seek, and ye shall find;
Knock, and it shall be opened unto you.

MATTHEW 7:7

If by strength is meant brute strength,
then, indeed, is woman less brute than man.

If by strength is meant moral power,
then woman is immeasurably man's superior.

If nonviolence is the law of our being,
the future is with women.

GANDHI

SOURCES

Prologue

"I have called on the Goddess and found her within myself": Bradley, Marion Zimmer. *The mists of Avalon*. NY: Ballantine Books, 1984, p. 19. Print.

1: The Quest

7   "Aphrodite just kept smiling": Smith, Lisa Jane. *Spellbinder*. New York, NY: Pocket Books, 1996. Print.

SO FAR AWAY

10   Ken Wilber: Wilber speaking to a gathering at a private home in Marin County, CA, 1997.

16   the root word "ken," or a close derivation of it, in several languages, including German: *Wiktionary, The Free Dictionary*. 20 Sep 2016, 14:51 UTC. 19 Nov 2016. Web. <https://en.wiktionary.org/wiki/kennen>

16   English, and Scottish, and it means "to know," or "consciousness": "ken." *Oxford Living Dictionaries*. 19 Nov 2016. Web. <https://en.oxforddictionaries.com/definition/us/ken>

16   he saw all of his waking life to be dreamlike: Although Jung never said exactly those words in his writings, his work is filled with the power

of this metaphor. See: Jung, C, G.; Aniela Jaffé, Ed. *Memories, dreams, reflections.* New York, NY: Vintage Books, 1989. Print.

In a similar way, Tibetan Buddhism also considers life to be like a dream. For example, see: Sogyal Rinpoche; Patrick Gaffney and Andrew Harvey, Eds. *The Tibetan book of living and dying.* New York, NY: HarperCollins, 1993, pp. 25-27. Print.

17   I reached for my *Medicine Cards*: Although there is some controversy over the exact practices that Native Americans have used with animals, it is the metaphors that are powerful, and, regardless of their historical accuracy, they make for "good medicine" for self-exploration.

Here is the book-and-card set I have: Sams, Jamie and David Carson; illustrations by Angela Werneke. *Medicine cards: The discovery of power through the ways of animals.* Rochester, VT: Bear & Company, 1988. Print. "Cast out deception": p. 120, and "to see right through": p. 122.

ROOF OF THE WORLD

21   "But I am not going to live forever": Hurt, William. "Biography." *Internet Movie Database.* 19 Nov 2016, 22:30. Web. <http://www.imdb.com/name/nm0000458/bio?ref_=nm_ov_bio_sm#quotes>

22   I recalled that the mage Merlin had morphed him into animals: Many renditions of this story of Merlin morphing a young King Arthur into animals exist. One of my favorites is this: White, Terence Hanbury. *The once and future king.* New York, NY: Penguin Books, 1939. Print.

24   El Niño was in full swing: Lin, Rong-Gong II, and Mai-Duc, Christine. "The great El Niño of 1997-98, and what it means for the winter to come." 22 Aug 2015, 9:01am. *Los Angeles Times.* 19 Nov 2016, 22:30. Web. <http://www.latimes.com/local/california/la-me-0822-el-nino-1997-20150822-story.html>

25   blissfully stride off a cliff: Campbell, Joseph (some chapters), and Richards, Robert. *Tarot revelations.* San Anselmo, CA: Vernal Equinox Press, 1987. Print.

For example, "to insights such as may lead, in the end, to the joy in wisdom of THE FOOL." See also: "The fool (tarot card)." *Wikipedia, The Free Encyclopedia.* 21 Nov 2016. Web. <https://en.wikipedia.org/wiki/The_Fool_(Tarot_card)>

25   depths of the psyche: Campbell, Joseph. *The hero with a thousand faces.* New York, NY: Pantheon, 1949. Print. (New World Library, 2008 Ed. Print.)

DECLARATION OF POWER

29   "Traveling outgrows its motives": Bouvier, Nicolas. *The way of the world.* New York, NY: New York Review Books, 2007, p. 13. Print.

31   Namtso is remarkable with its huge size: Namtso, a saltwater lake, is one of the largest lakes in Tibet and China. See: Wikipedia Contributors. "Namtso." *Wikipedia, The Free Encyclopedia.* 4 Oct 2016. 19 Nov 2016. Web. <https://en.wikipedia.org/wiki/Namtso>

32   Then I prostrated devoutly, in the traditional Tibetan way: a cultural and symbolic religious act of respect and ego submission common in Tibet and within Buddhism in general.

     For example, see: Wikipedia Contributors. "Prostration (Buddhism)." *Wikipedia, The Free Encyclopedia.* 17 Nov 2016. 19 Nov 2016, 22:30. Web. <https://en.wikipedia.org/wiki/Prostration_(Buddhism)>

     See also: Shih, Sun-Inn. "Tibetan Prostration." *Tibet Mandala.* 19 Nov 2016, 22:30. Web. <http://www.kalachakra.org/articles/prostration. shtml>

32   create a special series of tasks: In the myth, Psyche is given tasks by Venus/Aphrodite.

     To read more, see: Johnson, Robert A. *She: Understanding feminine psychology.* New York, NY: HarperCollins, 1989. Print.

DARKNESS

35   When the gods wish to punish us: Wilde, Oscar. *An ideal husband.* Mineola, NY: Dover Publications, 1895, Act II, p. 28. Print. (2001 Ed. Print.)

35   "zee book" Alive: Read, Piers Paul. *Alive: The story of the Andes survivors.* New York, NY: Lippincott, 1974. Print.

     An American film adapted from Read's book and bearing the same title was released in 1993. It documents the events of Uruguayan Air Force Flight 571, a charter flight that crashed in the snow-laden Andes while carrying a Uruguayan rugby team, whose survivors had to resort to cannibalism in order to survive.

THE FALL

43   Half gods are worshipped in wine and flowers: Hurston, Zora Neale. *Their eyes were watching God.* New York, NY: HarperCollins, 1937, p. 170. Print.

45   is called countertransference: Wikipedia Contributors. "Countertransference." *Wikipedia, The Free Encyclopedia.* 2 Sep 2016, 14:51 UTC. 19 Nov 2016. Web.

        <https://en.wikipedia.org/wiki/Countertransference>

        In particular, see "personal countertransference" and compare that with "diagnostic response" (and even the more recent theory of "embodied countertransference").

        For a social worker's perspective on the value of self-awareness in psychotherapy, see: Urdang, Esther. "Awareness of self—a critical tool." *Social Work Education.* Vol. 29, No. 5, August 2010, pp. 523-539. 19 Nov 2016, 22:30. Web. <https://www.bu.edu/ssw/files/2010/10/Awareness-of-Self-A-Critical-Tool.pdf>

2: Hungry Ghost

51   "Do you know the most surprising thing about divorce?": Dir. and Writ. Wells, Audrey. "Under the Tuscan Sun." Auth. Mayes, Frances. *Script-O-Rama.* "Script – Dialogue Transcript." Diane Lane, as Frances. 19 Nov 2016, 22:30. Web. <http://www.script-o-rama.com/movie_scripts/u/under-the-tuscan-sun-script-transcript.html>

        See also: Under the Tuscan Sun. "Quotes." *Internet Movie Database.* 19 Nov 2016, 22:30. Web. <http://www.imdb.com/title/tt0328589/quotes>

BARDO

56   I met with a nun named Ani: Pronounced AH-nee, the Tibetan word ani means nun.

56   because every ani-la: Pronounced AH-nee-lah, the suffix la is an affectionate term or an epithet that's often appended to Tibetan first names, surnames, and even some titles. The word means honored or dear, so calling Ani Karen ani-la, for example, was similar to addressing her as "my dear nun."

This suffix is used liberally in spoken Tibetan; for example, the same practice holds true with the Tibetan word ama, which means mother. When speaking to or about any particular mother, la is frequently used to form the term ama-la or amala. Similarly, I often used this with Tashi, and so I would call her Tashi-la.

56   woman with a mala: The Sanskrit word mala means "garland," and it constitutes a string of prayer beads somewhat similar to a rosary and, for Buddhists, is generally composed of 108 or 111 beads strung together and used to recite and count mantras. While malas are commonly used in several spiritual or religious traditions, in the Tibetan Buddhist context a mantra is a Sanskrit or Tibetan phrase or a series of syllables that carry spiritual meaning and potency, and these mantras are often repeated over and over.

57   Bardo? I'm in a bardo: Sogyal Rinpoche; Patrick Gaffney and Andrew Harvey, Eds. *The Tibetan book of living and dying.* New York, NY: HarperCollins, 1993. Print.

57   "The word 'bardo' is commonly said to": Ibid, p. 11.

58   Scrooge goes through a bardo one night: Dickens, Charles. *A Christmas carol.* London, UK: Chapman and Hall, 1843. Print.

58   a bardo occurs in the movie: *The Matrix.* Dir. Andy Wachowski and Larry Wachowski. Warner Bros. Pictures, 1999. DVD. Also see: Wachowski, Andy and Larry Wachowski. "The Matrix." *Internet Movie Script Database.* 19 Nov 2016, 22:30. Web. <http://www.imsdb.com/scripts/Matrix,-The.html>

(Note: Some significant moments in the movie do not match this script. Obviously, if this is the final written script, the actual words spoken were altered somewhat during the final film shoot.)

59   Psyche had fallen in love with Eros: Johnson, Robert A. *She: Understanding feminine psychology.* New York, NY: HarperCollins, 1989. Print.

59   dinner in Lhasa with fellow traveler Glenn Mullin: <http://glennmullin.com>

60   some Tibetan Buddhist practices are done in graveyards: See: Wikipedia Contributors. "Chöd." *Wikipedia, The Free Encyclopedia.* 3 Nov 2016. 19 Nov 2016, 22:30. Web. <https://en.wikipedia.org/wiki/Ch%C3%B6d>

62   bardo that typically precedes rebirth: In this particular bardo after one's

death, Tibetan Buddhists believe there is a heightened ability, and that it is an opportune time for one's ego to be recognized as illusory, and for one's true nature to be recognized.

In the Buddhist tradition, one learns during one's life, over time, to recognize the manifestations of ego and leave them, and ultimately the ego itself, at the door, so to speak. Ego, in this context, entails all the thoughts, or concepts, one has around oneself and others: fears involving this life; fears concerning one's own survival as well as one's own death; one's attachment to any thoughts and fears others may hold, especially at the time of death, and so on. Essentially, the ego encompasses all one's concepts of the self, of others, and of phenomena itself, including the belief that one is somehow solid, permanent, and separate. If, due to not having achieved a stable recognition of one's true nature (buddha nature), one is unable to let go of concepts, then one will continue to wander, cycle after cycle, on samsara's wheel, until one is able to overcome this illusion with the recognition of unfettered, spacious awareness.

Regarding the phrase "samsara's wheel" in this end note: samsara is a Sanskrit word that is translated in Tibetan as korwa or kora, which means "to circle" or "turn around." Samsara is a description of what Buddhism and other Eastern religious and spiritual traditions see as the almost endless-seeming cycle of existence as one is reborn over-and-over again until one attains complete enlightenment or Buddhahood. See also: <http://rywiki.tsadra.org/index.php/%27khor_ ba>

62   "But when I heard the storm": Muir, John and Terry Gifford. *John Muir: His life and letters and other writings.* London, UK: Bâton Wicks Publications, 1996. Print; Seattle, WA: Mountaineers Books, 1996. Print.

62   Japanese Zen master Shido Bunan had said: Bunan's words are paraphrased here from the translation: Shibayama, Zenkei. *A flower does not talk: Zen essays.* Rutland, VT: Charles E. Tuttle Co., 1970. Print.

63   Psyche's final task: See: Wikipedia Contributors. "Cupid and Psyche." *Wikipedia, The Free Encyclopedia.* 14 Nov 2016. 19 Nov 2016, 22:30. Web. <https://en.wikipedia.org/wiki/Cupid_and_Psyche#Psyche_and_ the_underworld>

63   "the valley of the shadow of death": Psalm 23:4. <http://biblehub.com/ psalms/23-4.htm>

64 Tashi's mother was a great niece of the 13th Dalai Lama: Author's personal notes.

See also: Yuthok, Dorje Yudon; Michael Harlin, Trans and Ed. *House of the turquoise roof.* Ithaca, NY: Snow Lion, 1995. Print.

68 one of two basic features of a labyrinth: See: Artress, Lauren. *Walking a sacred path: Rediscovering the labyrinth as a spiritual practice.* New York, NY: Riverhead Books, 2006. Print.

See also: Attali, Jacques. *The labyrinth in culture and society: Pathways to wisdom.* Berkeley, CA: North Atlantic Books, 1999. Print.

SACRIFICE

71 "I have been in Sorrow's kitchen": Hurston, Zora Neale. *Dust tracks on a road.* New York, NY: Harper Perennial Modern Classics, 2006. Print.

75/121. archetypal experience from the collective unconscious: Jung developed the term collective unconscious, see: Wikipedia Contributors. "Collective unconscious." *Wikipedia, The Free Encyclopedia.* 26 Oct 2016. 19 Nov 2016, 22:30. Web. <https://en.wikipedia.org/wiki/Collective_unconscious>

See also: Jung, C. G., R. F. C. Hull, and Gerhard Adler. *The archetypes and the collective unconscious.* Princeton, NJ: Princeton University Press, 1969. Print.

74 "Barn's burnt down": Masahide, Mizuta in Stryk, Lucien, and Takashi Ikemoto. *Zen poetry: Let the spring breeze enter.* New York, NY: Grove Press, 1995, p. 77. Print.

3: Victim to Pilgrim

77 "Ged stood for a long while": Le Guin, Ursula K. *A wizard of Earthsea.* New York, NY: Houghton Mifflin, 1968, p. 39.

CALL OF THE CONCH

83 "Milarepa stew": For a rather extensive account of Milarepa's life, including his diet of nettle stew, see: <http://www.thranguhk.org/buddhism/en_milarepa.html> and reference the subheading "Ascetic Diet of Nettles."

84   traditional dakini knife: You can access a description and a picture of this ceremonial knife (Tib. drigug) at: <https://en.wikipedia.org/wiki/Kartika_(knife)>

85   Reminded me of one of my favorite chapters: Lewis, C. S. *The voyage of the dawn treader.* London, UK: Geoffrey Bles, 1952. Print.

89   iconic spiral depicted in cave paintings: for more extensive details about the labyrinth as a spiral, see: <http://library.ciis.edu/resources/regenesis/labryrinth_10_08.pdf>

SOLIDARITY

91   "Sorrows are the rags of old clothes": Rumi, Jalal ad-Din; Coleman Barks, Trans. *The essential Rumi.* San Francisco, CA: Harper, 1997. Used with permission.

92   CIF: For more details about the Creative Initiative Foundation and related groups, see: <http://www.globalcommunity.org/fgcHistory.pdf>

103   instead of taking meds: If it is possible to work through an issue without medication, one can experience pain that may be important to feel. This method can be an effective way to deal with tough experiences. However, this does not mean that medication is necessarily contraindicated in any particular case. In fact, to the contrary: in some cases, taking medication can be the only way to survive. If you are considering options around your use of medicine for psychological help for depression or other significant emotional distress, please consult a licensed professional with whom you can jointly work. Doing so may save your life.

4: Heart of the Matter

107   "A thousand half-loves": Rumi, Jalal ad-Din; Coleman Barks, Trans. *The essential Rumi.* San Francisco, CA: Harper, 1997. Used with permission.

BLACK BOX

110   Nothing can exist: For some (fourth grade-level) science on black holes, see <http://www.nasa.gov/audience/forstudents/k-4/stories/nasa-knows/what-is-a-black-hole-k4.html>

111   Mandalas are universal designs: Jung speaks about mandalas in Jung, C. G.; Aniela Jaffé, Ed.; Richard and Clara Winston, Trans. *Memories, dreams, reflections.* New York, NY: Vintage Books, 1989. Print.

111   fractal geometry discussion group: See: Mandelbrot, Benoit B. *The fractal geometry of nature.* San Francisco, CA: W. H. Freeman, 1982. Print.

112   "Do you know about the black cube": For more details, see: Hurtak, J. J. *The book of knowledge: The keys of Enoch.* Los Gatos, CA: Academy for Future Science, 1996. Print.

112   "It's related to the Kabbalistic cube": See: Townley, Kevin. *The cube of space: Container of creation.* Boulder, CO and Montreal, QC: Archive Press Editions Le Chaos, 1993. Print.

112   about the Jewish ceremony: Wikipedia Contributors. "Tefillin." *Wikipedia, The Free Encyclopedia.* 20 Oct 2016. 19 Nov 2016, 22:30. Web. <https://en.wikipedia.org/wiki/Tefillin>

112   "It's called The Hurricane": "The Hurricane." *Internet Movie Database.* 19 Nov 2016. Web. <http://www.imdb.com/title/tt0174856>

114   my heart was the optic nerve: Advanced Tibetan Buddhist practitioners have told me that this is actually one of the deepest, highest of teachings in the esoteric tantric teachings, this connection between the optic nerve and one's heart and bloodstream and that advanced meditation practices in these schools make use of this connection. (See the Dzogchen or Atiyoga teachings and speak to a qualified Tibetan Buddhist lama for more details. There is very little information available on this topic that makes much sense without having the help of a lama or personal teacher. So if you want to learn more, it is highly recommended that you investigate and carefully choose a qualified lama to guide you.)

115   "The earth was formless and void": Genesis 1:1, see: <http://biblehub. com/genesis/1-1.htm>

116   Is that what is meant by the mustard seed of faith: Matthew 17:20, see: <http://biblehub.com/matthew/17-20.htm>

GRASPING SELF

119   "No one can make you feel inferior": Eleanor Roosevelt was an inspiring woman. This aphorism may well be apocryphal, though it seems clear that she would have approved of its attribution to her—or maybe

did approve of it during her lifetime. See: "No one can make you feel inferior without your consent." *Quote Investigator.* 19 Nov 2016. <http://quoteinvestigator.com/2012/04/30/no-one-inferior/>

120   I think a dictionary definition would say: "Ego." *Merriam-Webster Online.* 2012a. <http://www.merriam-webster.com/dictionary/ego>

120   Freud believed the ego: "Id, ego, and super-ego." *Wikipedia, The Free Encyclopedia.* 17 Nov 2016. 19 Nov 2016, 22:30. Web. <https://en.wikipedia.org/w/index.php?title=Id,_ego_and_super-ego&oldid=750030947>

120   Jung believed the ego: Abrams, Jeremiah, and Connie Zweig. *Meeting the shadow: The hidden power of the dark side of human nature.* Los Angeles, CA and New York, NY: J.P. Tarcher. Distributed by St. Martin's Press, 1991, p. 24. Quoting John Sanford on Jungian psychology.

122   The word for ego in Tibetan is dak dzin: "Self-grasping" *Rigpa Shedra, RigpaWiki.* 24 Jan 2011. 19 Nov 2016, 22:30. Web. <http://www.rigpawiki.org/index.php?title=Self-grasping>

THE ENEMY

125   "So many people throughout my life have told me who I am": Hatayama, Amythyst. *The spiritual feminist.* Blue Ridge Summit, PA: John Hunt Publishing (Moon Books), 2015. Print.

125   a woman named Esperide: pronounced ess-PAIR-ih-day

125   a community in Italy called Damanhur: See the Federation of Damanhur: <http://www.damanhur.org>

128   The main character is Anansel: pronounced AHN-ahn-sell.

128   But the real bake-my-noodle truth: this phrase was taken from the movie *The Matrix*, op. cit., though it didn't likely originate there.

129   "People who go about seeking to change the world": Walker, Alice. *Anything we love can be saved: A writer's activism.* New York, NY: Random House, 1997. Print.

THE PROJECTOR

131   "The most potent weapon in the hands of the oppressor": Biko, Steve; Aelred Stubbs, Ed. *I write what I like.* New York, NY: Harper & Row, 1979. Print.

135   That women are whores. That they're madonnas: See: Wikipedia Contributors. "Madonna-whore complex." *Wikipedia, The Free Encyclopedia.* 15 Nov 2016. 19 Nov 2016, 22:30. Web. <https://en.wikipedia.org/wiki/Madonna%E2%80%93whore_complex>

138   "It's textbook," Andrea said: *DSM 5: Diagnostic and statistical manual of mental disorders, 5th ed.*; for example, see narcissistic personality disorder: <http://www.theravive.com/therapedia/Narcissistic-Personality-Disorder-DSM--5-301.81-(F60.81)>; anti-social personality disorder: <http://www.theravive.com/therapedia/Antisocial-Personality-Disorder-DSM--5-301.7-(F60.2)>

INTERNALIZED MISOGYNY

145   "Then when you know better, do better": Oprah Winfrey's paraphrasing of Maya Angelou's words, see that rendition at <https://youtu.be/watch?v=fx447ShQLeE> in particular, starting here: <https://youtu.be/fx447ShQLeE?t=1m55s>. Although Angelou is commonly credited with saying this, or something very similar, her exact words, and the original source or context, remain unverified at the time of this printing.

146   "Winnicott's work on subjective omnipotence": Winnicott, D. W. *The maturational processes and the facilitating environment: Studies in the theory of emotional development.* Madison, CT: International Universities Press, 1996. Print.

146   "Object relations at this level is not my area of expertise": See: Wikipedia Contributors. "Object relations theory." *Wikipedia, The Free Encyclopedia.* 20 Oct 2016. 19 Nov 2016, 22:30. Web. <https://en.wikipedia.org/wiki/Object_relations_theory>

See also: Wikipedia Contributors. "Attachment theory." *Wikipedia, The Free Encyclopedia.* 7 Nov 2016. 19 Nov 2016, 22:30. Web. <https://en.wikipedia.org/wiki/Attachment_theory>

148   The term "collective intelligence": See: Jaworski, Joseph. *Synchronicity: The inner path of leadership*, 2nd Ed. San Francisco: Berrett-Koehler Publishers, 2011. Print.

See also: Bohm, David, and Lee Nichol. *On dialogue.* London, UK and New York, NY: Routledge, 2004. Print.

Also, here is a cautionary tale told by Joseph Jaworski regarding working on yourself first, before trying to harness collective or group intelligence: <https://www.youtube.com/watch?v=l46RerlI5V0>

HER STORY

153 "The hatred of women affects us in ways": Holland, Jack. *Misogyny: The world's oldest prejudice.* New York: Carroll & Graf Publishers (now an imprint of Perseus Books Group). Distributed by Publishers Group West, 2006, p. 11. Print.

154 multigenerational (or family) transmission process: See: McGoldrick, Monica, and Kenneth V. Hardy. *Re-visioning family therapy: Race, culture, and gender in clinical practice, 2nd ed.* New York, NY: Guilford Press, 2008. Print.

159 George and Joseph Herrick: Wikipedia Contributors. "Joseph Herrick." *Wikipedia, The Free Encyclopedia.* 14 Jun 2016. 19 Nov 2016, 22:30. Web. <https://en.wikipedia.org/wiki/Joseph_Herrick> (Note: The page about George is sparse and less referenced than Joseph's, but a link to the page for George appears on the page for Joseph, which is linked above.)

160 Similar horrors had been going on for centuries in Europe: Kors, Alan C., and Edward Peters, Eds. *Witchcraft in europe, 400-1700: A documentary history, 2nd ed.* Philadelphia, PA: University of Pennsylvania Press, 2001. Print.

160 It is estimated that 75 to 80 percent of those killed were women: Barstow, Anne L. *Witchcraze: A new history of the European witch hunts.* San Francisco, CA: Pandora, 1994. Print.

161 "women's proneness to lust and therefore to demonic temptation": Kors, Alan C., and Edward Peters, Eds. *Witchcraft in Europe, 400-1700: A documentary history, 2nd ed.* Philadelphia, PA: University of Pennsylvania Press, 2001, p. 36. Print.

161 The Herrick family tree: See: Herrick, George and Joseph Herrick. Op. cit.

162 the minute a woman had sex, she relinquished her power: See: Gilmore, David D. *Misogyny: The male malady.* Philadelphia, PA: University of Pennsylvania Press, 2001. Print.

See also the following works:

Holland, Jack. *Misogyny: The world's oldest prejudice.* New York, NY: Carroll & Graf Publishers (now an imprint of Perseus Books Group). Distributed by Publishers Group West, 2006. Print.

Lerner, Gerda. *The creation of feminist consciousness: From the Middle Ages to eighteen-seventy.* New York, NY: Oxford University Press, 1993. Print.

Rogers, Katharine M. *The troublesome helpmate: A history of misogyny in literature.* Seattle, WA and London, UK: University of Washington Press, 1968. Print.

Shlain, Leonard. *The alphabet versus the goddess: The conflict between word and image.* New York, NY: Penguin/Arkana, 1999. Print.

Stone, Merlin. *When God was a woman.* New York, NY: Harcourt Brace Jovanovich, 1978. Print.

162   "Then be not coy, but use your time": Herrick, Robert; F. W. Moorman, Ed. *The poetical works of Robert Herrick.* UK: Oxford University Press, 1915, p. 84. Print.

     See also: Wikipedia contributors. "To the Virgins, to Make Much of Time." *Wikipedia, The Free Encyclopedia.* 22 Sep 2016. Web. <https://en.wikipedia.org/wiki/To_the_Virgins,_to_Make_Much_of_Time>

163   Whoever a woman married determined her safety: See: Holland, Jack. Op. cit.

165   Eve had committed this sinful act out of a lack of personal control and will: See: Wikipedia contributors. "Augustine of Hippo." *Wikipedia, The Free Encyclopedia.* 20 Nov 2016. Web. <https://en.wikipedia.org/wiki/Augustine_of_Hippo#Sexuality>

167   She may have arisen even earlier in herstory: See: Budin, Stephanie L. "A Reconsideration of the Aphrodite-Ashtart Syncretism." *Numen, vol. 51,* No. 2, 2004, pp. 95–145. <http://www.jstor.org/stable/3270523>

168   "As long as we are on earth, the love that unites us": See: Merton, Thomas. *New seeds of contemplation.* New York, NY: New Directions (paperbook: 1091), 2007, p. 72. Print.

THE MIRROR

171   "One does not become enlightened": See: Jung, C. G. *Psychology and alchemy (Collected works of C. G. Jung, vol. 12).* Princeton, NJ: Princeton University Press, 1968, p. 99. Print.

171   "Internalized misogyny explains some of women's psychology": See: Daleo, Dina, and Michele Riggs, *Internalized misogyny: Conceptu-*

alizations and implications. Doctoral dissertation, Los Angeles, CA: California School of Professional Psychology, 1996. Print.

172 learned helplessness: See: Walker, Lenore E. *The battered woman.* New York, NY: Harper & Row, 1979. Print.

172 post-traumatic stress disorder: *DSM-5: Diagnostic and statistical manual of mental disorders, 5th ed.*; for example: <http://www.theravive. com/therapedia/Posttraumatic-Stress-Disorder-(PTSD)-DSM--5-309.81-(F43.10)> Web.

172 dependent personality disorder: *DSM-5: Diagnostic and statistical manual of mental disorders, 5th ed.*; for example: <http://www.theravive.com/ther apedia/Dependent-Personality-Disorder-DSM--5-301.6-(F60.7)> Web.

INTERVENTION

175 "An integrated individual is one who": de Castillejo, Irene C. *Knowing woman: A feminine psychology.* New York, NY: Harper & Row, 1974, pp. 29–30. Print.

176 I pulled out a Thomas Merton book of Gandhi's writings: Gandhi, Mo-handas; Thomas Merton, Ed. *Gandhi on non-violence: Selected texts from Mohandas K. Gandhi's non-violence in peace and war.* New York, NY: New Directions, 1965. Print.

176 "You must, in the nature of things, humiliate us to control us": Briley, John. "Gandhi" *Screenplays for You.* Ben Kingsley as Gandhi, speaking to the British. 19 Nov 2016, 22:30. Web. <http://sfy.ru/?script=gandhi>

176 It stems from the word "humus": "Humiliate." *Merriam-Webster Online.* 2012a. Web. <http://www.merriam-webster.com/dictionary/humiliate>

176 I could see what Gandhi was faced with: Kibriya, Mazhar. *Gandhi and Indian freedom struggle.* New Delhi, India: APH Publishing Corpo-ration, 1999.

177 if your peers during your teenage years shame you: See: Bradshaw, John. *Healing the shame that binds you.* Deerfield Beach, FL: Health Commu-nications, Inc., 1988.

See also: Erikson H., Erik. *Childhood and society.* New York, NY: W. W. Norton & Company Inc., 1993.

178 "Man's nature is not essentially evil": See: Gandhi, Mahatma. *Collected*

works, vol. 68. Publications Division, Ministry of Information and Broadcasting, Government of India, 1977, p. 57. Print.

178   I was reading a book by the relationship aficionado: Hendrix, Harville. *Keeping the love you find: A personal guide.* New York, NY: Pocket Books, 1992. Print.

All of the books by Hendrix on his Imago theory are excellent, by the way.

179   "Gandhi was probably the first person in history to lift the love ethic of Jesus above mere interaction": See: King, Martin L.; Clayborne Carson, Ed. *The autobiography of Martin Luther King, Jr.* New York, NY: Intellectual Properties Management in association with Warner Books, 1998, p. 24. Print.

179   "Human salvation lies in the hands of the creatively maladjusted": King, Martin L., Jr., and Coretta S. King. *Strength to love.* Minneapolis, MN: Fortress, 2010, p. 18. Print.

180   the usual fight response of the lizard-like brain: Wikipedia Contributors. "Triune Brain." *Wikipedia, The Free Encyclopedia.* 13 Nov 2016. Web. <https://en.wikipedia.org/wiki/Triune_brain#Reptilian_complex>

Note that modern neuroscience has now gone far beyond the simple triune brain hypothesis, but for my purposes here it provides a good enough approximation to explain the reptilian-type responses I'm describing.

180   largest fountain on the West Coast: See: Wikipedia Contributors. "Yerba Buena Gardens." *Wikipedia, The Free Encyclopedia.* 13 Nov 2016. Web. <https://en.wikipedia.org/wiki/Yerba_Buena_Gardens#Public_art>

See also: <http://www.artandarchitecture-sf.com/martin-luther-king-memorial.html>

181   My father spoke at the gathering: He spoke outdoors, on the steps of the Stanford Memorial Church, as my mother recollected recently. See: <http://stanforddailyarchive.com/cgi-bin/stanford?a=d&d=stanford19680408-01.1.4&e=-------en-20--1--txt-txIN-------#>

181   "No, no, we are not satisfied, and we will not be satisfied until justice rolls down": <http://news.bbc.co.uk/2/hi/americas/3170387.stm>

See also the following links:

Wikipedia Contributors. "I have a dream." *Wikipedia, The Free Encyclopedia.* 5 Nov 2016. 19 Nov 2016, 22:30. Web. <https://en.wikipedia.org/wiki/I_Have_a_Dream>

Wikipedia Contributors. "March on Washington for jobs and freedom." Wikipedia, The Free Encyclopedia. 3 Nov 2016. 19 Nov 2016, 22:30. Web. <https://en.wikipedia.org/wiki/March_on_Washington_for_Jobs_and_Freedom>

182   In her work with the personality typology system called the Enneagram: See: Palmer, Helen. *The pocket enneagram: Understanding the 9 types of people.* San Francisco, CA: HarperSanFrancisco, 1995.

182   that corresponded to my vice of disengagement: Helen Palmer calls this "sloth." In an attempt to be more accessible to an audience that doesn't know the Enneagram, I've chosen the word disengagement, to mean a condition of "not trying," which involves a kind of laziness, or sloth.

WAKING UP APHRODITE

185   "I have learned over the years that when one's mind is made up": See: Parks, Rosa, and Gregory J. Reed. *Quiet strength: The faith, the hope, and the heart of a woman who changed a nation.* Grand Rapids, MI: Zondervan Publishing House, 1994, p. 17. Print.

186   "No, no, we . . . will not be satisfied until justice rolls down": partial quote from Martin Luther King, Jr. speech "I have a dream," delivered at March on Washington for jobs and freedom. Op. cit.

189   "How could we forget those ancient myths": Rilke, Rainer M. *Letters to a young poet.* New York, NY and London, UK: W. W. Norton & Co., 1993, p. 69. Print.

5: Matter in Motion

191   "Magic is the art of changing consciousness at will": Starhawk (paraphrasing Dion Fortune). *The fifth sacred thing.* New York, NY: Bantam Books, 1993, p. 152. Print.

CALLED

197   "We are volcanoes": Le Guin, Ursula K. "Commencement." Bryn Mawr College, 1986, Bryn Mawr, PA. Commencement Address.

RIPPLES

209   "Each time a man stands up for an ideal": Kennedy, Robert F.: <http://www.rfksafilm.org/html/speeches/unicape.php> See also: <http://www.npr.org/sections/thetwo-way/2013/06/30/197342656/looking-back-rfks-ripple-of-hope-speech-in-south-africa>

VIRTUE

217   "If you want to make peace": "Moshe Dayan." *Wikiquote.* 29 Oct 2016, 05:49 UTC. 22 Nov 2016. Web. <https://en.wikiquote.org/wiki/Moshe_Dayan>

6: Release

221   "The only thing that makes life possible": Le Guin, Ursula K. *The left hand of darkness.* New York: Ace Books, 1976, p. 70. Print.

See also: "Ursula K. Le Guin." *Wikiquote.* 10 Nov 2016, 15:18 UTC. 22 Nov 2016. Web. <https://en.wikiquote.org/wiki/Ursula_K._Le_Guin#The_Left_Hand_of_Darkness_.281969.29>

EXCHANGE

223   Thirteen, in the context of my new-age religious upbringing, was considered a mystical number: See: <http://rateyourmusic.com/release/album/creative_initiative_foundation/thirteen_is_a_mystical_number>

224   consists of thirteen moons: 28 x 13 = 364 days, although only about thirty seven out of every one hundred years contain thirteen full moons. See also "A repressed lunar cult" here: Wikipedia Contributors. "13 (number)." *Wikipedia, The Free Encyclopedia.* 22 Nov 2016. Web. <https://en.wikipedia.org/wiki/13_(number)#Unlucky_13>

225   "No more talk of darkness": See: <https://www.youtube.com/watch?v=uxs7qevmy50>

CHUCK'S PEARLS

231   "We work on ourselves, then, in order to help others": Dass, Ram, and Paul Gorman. *How can I help? Stories and reflections on service.* New York, NY: Knopf, 1985, p. 224. Print.

231   ceremonial silk scarf, a khata: Wikipedia Contributors. "Khata." *Wikipedia, The Free Encyclopedia.* 22 Aug 2016. 19 Nov 2016, 22:30. Web. <https://en.wikipedia.org/wiki/Khata>

233   how she'd followed *The Tibetan Book of Living and Dying*: Sogyal Rinpoche; Patrick Gaffney, and Andrew Harvey. Op. cit.

233   Tibetan Book of the Dead: Wikipedia Contributors. "Bardo Thodol." *Wikipedia, The Free Encyclopedia.* 14 Nov 2016. 19 Nov 2016, 22:30. Web. <https://en.wikipedia.org/wiki/Bardo_Thodol>

Among many English translations of this book, which is known in the Tibetan tradition as a treasure (Tib. *terma*) revealed by Karma Lingpa, this recent and well-regarded rendition is the first translation of the complete text. Coleman, Graham, Trans.; Thupten Jinpa and Gyurme Dorje, Eds.; commentary by Gyatso, Tenzin, His Holiness the 14th Dalai Lama and translators; by Karma-gli-pa, et al. *The Tibetan book of the dead* [English title]: *The great liberation by hearing in the intermediate states* [English translation of Tibetan title]. New York, NY: Penguin, 2007. Print. See: <http://a.co/1hRvl0U>

A MOST UNEXPECTED PLACE

237   "Of what is the body made": Leonard, George. *The silent pulse: A search for the perfect rhythm that exists in each of us.* Layton, UT: Gibbs Smith, 2006, p. 40. Print.

237   Email and quotes from Carol reproduced with permission.

Epilogue

239   "Then you will see it is not the spoon that bends, it is only one's self": *The Matrix.* Dir. Andy Wachowski and Larry Wachowski. Op. cit.

244   "Ask, and it shall be given you": See: <http://biblehub.com/matthew/7-7.htm>

245   "If by strength is meant brute strength": Gandhi, Mohandas. *All men are brothers: Autobiographical reflections.* New York, NY: Bloomsbury, 2013, p. 173. Print.

SPECIAL THANKS

Co-stars in the book
Andrea Urton, Ani Karen, Barbara Findeisen, Bufalo, Carol Misseldine,
Charles Kagochi, Daniel Kottke, Daniel Potter, Denise Rabius, Esperide
Ananas, Georgia Dow, Glenn Mullin, Hannah Herrick, Helen Caldicott,
Helen Palmer, Joel Rosenberg, Kate Wolf-Pizor, Marilyn Nyborg,
Megan Prelinger, Michael Axelman, Nancy Harris, Pat Moretti, Rachael
Vaughan, Randall Braun, Sandy Gove, Steve Omohundro, Sue Staley,
and members of my dad's men's group.

Readers and Brainstormers
Adam Dorsay, Amber Rae, Cat Coward, Charmayne Kilcup, Christine Moen,
David and Elena Johnston, Finbar Maxwell, Forrest Bennett,
Gentry Underwood, Gilles Bekaert, Helena Price, John Richardson, Kate
Wolf-Pizor, Laura Griffiths, Lynn Fielder, Mary Cunnane, Mary Ellen
O'Neill, Rachael Vaughan, Susan Esterly, Velvet Henderson, Yeshi Neumann,
and Zandra Kaufman.

Inspirers
Alison Tucher, Carl Marsak, Chris Wiscavage, Foster Gamble, Gerald
Smith, Helen Peters, Jackie Hart, Jeff Melchor, Jill Mellick, Kathy Tam,
Kelly Lenton, Laura Jean Anderson, Lucy Wurtz, Majo Molfino, Michael
Kaufman, Monica McGuire, Neal Kruse, Ron Goettinger, Roslyn Braun,
Roy Gordon, Sergio Scales, Steve Rehmus, Suketu Mehta, Tim Silbaugh,
and Will Goldberg.

SPECIAL THANKS

Groups and Organizations
Creative Initiative Foundation, Damanhur,
Institute of Transpersonal Psychology,
my dad's men's group, and Peace Mind Dialogue.

Our Kickstarter Funders
Every one of you made publishing this book possible.
In particular, those who went above and beyond:
Adam Dorsay, Alison Tucher, Allison Garcia, Andrew Vilcsak, Annessa
Braymer, Artie Wu, Bea Herrick, Bernadette Cay, Bradford Cottel,
Brett & Betsy Cottel, Brian Lam, Brigit Kang, Carla Saunders, Cat Coward
& Tim Silbaugh, Craig Mod, David Lang, Enrique Allen, I'Lee & Tony
Hooker, Jared Erondu, Johnnie Manzari, Katie Walvatne, Kim Fusch,
Laura Brunow Miner, Lay-Leng Low, Maddie Callander,
Madelin Woods, Marilyn Nyborg, Nicole Systrom, Purvi Shah, Rachelle
Bilger, Rebecca Sinclair, Rick Louie, Robert Padbury, Roslyn Braun,
Roxanne Sutton, Stephanie Wolf, Susan Spinrad Esterly, Unnikrishna
Menon Damodaran, and Zandra & Michael Kaufman.

Family Members
My mother Bea Herrick, for her bravery and her
unconditional support, My mother-in-law Samara Kemp,
The Herricks & Harts, The Baileys & Hookers, The Kagochis,
The Cottels & Colls, The McGlashans, all of the ancestors,
and those no longer with us: Jim, Tashi, and Chuck.

For all those that I did not mention, you are a part
of me, even if forgotten! Forgive me.

Most of all
The star, my father: Jim Herrick, and
the team: Bradford Cottel & Elle Luna, "Go Team Go!"
I am free because you took your beloved hands and untied the
knots encasing my dreams. I am flying because of you.

*To Grace with the pink diapers at the Japanese Tea
Garden in 2016: this is for everything ahead!*

SUSIE HERRICK is a licensed psychotherapist, personality typology expert, former academic department chair and professor, certified mediator, trainer, consultant, and writer. She has taught, coached, and mentored over two thousand graduate students in counseling psychology. Learn more at susieherrick.com and aphroditeemerges.com.

ELLE LUNA is a painter, designer, and writer. She is the author of *The Crossroads of Should and Must: Find and Follow Your Passion* (Workman, 2015). She lives in San Francisco and on instagram.com/elleluna.